TOUCH THE PAIN

TOUCH THE PAIN

The Servant Church in the 21st Century

Bill McNamara

Library of Congress Number: 00-190791
ISBN #: Hardcover 0-7388-1997-2
Softcover 0-7388-1998-0

This book was printed in the United States of America.

Cover Design by O'Connell Associates

To order additional copies of this book, contact:
Xlibris Corporation
1-888-7-XLIBRIS
www.Xlibris.com
Orders@Xlibris.com

CONTENTS

BIOGRAPHY

Bill McNamara's multifaceted personal history is a tapestry. The integrity and strength you can feel in the "touch" are provided by the continuous threads of family community, and Jesus. The vibrantly personal colors you can see woven through this tapestry are his discipline, steadfastness, and rich, gentle humor.

Born in Boston, Massachusetts, Bill has been married for more than 56 years to his wife Angela; is father to eight, grandfather to twenty one [so far!] and friend and fatherly adviser to countless others, The commitment and counsel he offers to his extended family provides both roots and inspiration.

His covenant with country and family have been consistently demonstrated in significant accomplishments. A graduate of the United States Naval Flight School, Bill served as a World War II pilot and Captain in the U.S. Marine Corps. During his 37-year career in retail management, he advanced to department store senior executive, and shared his knowledge with others as a college business professor.

Bill's spiritual journey has been informed through education and enlivened by personal epiphanies. Educational awakenings came in many roles as both student and teacher: graduate of the Cardinal Cushing School of Theology for the Laity, religion teacher, parish lector, and Eucharistic minister. His social justice "knowledge" evolved through proactive advocacy as he touched the pain of human experiences in many roles: president of St. Vincent de Paul conferences, parish social ministry coordinator, Catholic Charities Director in the Diocese of Rockville Centre, founding member of the Woodstock Business Conference, and Chairperson of the Catholic Campaign for Human Development Allocations Committee. Bill was the recipient of the Catholic Charities Caritas Award, and was also recognized when a Parish Social Ministry Center was named in his honor.

As an author, Bill has developed several social justice curriculums for workshops and home study for deacons and laity. His prior writings include "Truth, Love, and Change" [social justice according to the Gospel of Luke], and regular articles in the diocesan monthly Passage.

In "Touch the Pain," Bill brings the conflicts of his pre and post Vatican Council experiences to life, and shares his perspective on church, charity, justice, and the challenges of living as a disciple of Jesus in a contemporary setting.

Joan McNamara

FOREWORD

We have spent our years like a sigh,
Seventy is the sum of our years or eighty if we are strong,
And most of them are fruitless toil, for they pass quickly and we drift away.

PS 90:9-10

This biblical lesson in life expectancy brings me to wonder why, if having passed my eightieth birthday, I don't just be still and wait to drift away to the place that Jesus has promised he has prepared for me as he takes me to himself[5] . Perhaps some words of the famous Irish writer, Samuel Beckett will help with the answer.

Perhaps my best years are gone,
But I would not want them back,
Not with the fire in me now.

After careers in the military for five years, the retail store business for thirty-seven, and for the past seventeen years in an active involvement in the Judeo/Christian Social Justice Doctrine and Teachings of our Church, I found myself on my eightieth birthday seriously reflecting on those latter years. It included the undeserved blessings that I have received from God over all of my lifetime. There are so many: very good mental and physical health, a loving and most supportive wife and

....

5 John 14:1-3

mother of our eight children, their spouses, twenty-one grandchildren, my own parents, relatives and friends,—and especially the relationships with the needy people who came to the Church carrying a cross and the men and women who had volunteered to suffer with them. As to the latter seventeen years, where was this energy coming from? Where did it seem to be centered? I'll answer the second question first.

During that period of time I have been sharing the Social Justice Teachings with hundreds of participants in parish settings. Yet, I experience a restlessness of concern over the endless number of individuals who state that they rarely or never hear the depth of the social justice message. Some of these people are in the pews and too many have left. It is with both of these groups—hungry and searching—that I share my testimony in recognition of an urgent need for the Church to be in solidarity with the poor in a commitment to justice.

Now to the first question, where was this energy coming from? It was and is the Spirit that will not allow this challenge to go away. It is the Spirit that is showing me the way as to how I should use my remaining days before I drift away. It is a divine energy that is calling everyone to encounter the poor as a Sacrament in demonstration of our love of God, our love of Jesus Christ crucified and our love for all of our brothers and sisters, especially those who are in the pain of poverty and oppression. It is the Spirit who reminds me that I am not a theologian in the academic sense of the word. Nor am I a gifted writer. I am a disciple of Jesus. I am being called to give this testimony as a witness to the true meaning of the word theology, namely, communication with God and with my neighbor about matters that are of God.

This is my testimony throughout. Any exceptions are so noted. This is the Jesus I know—where he is in my life—how I think he feels—what I believe he would say—where he would say it and how I believe he would act.

I leave the readers to the Jesus they know—where he is in their life—how they think he feels—what they believe he would say—where he would say it and how they think he would act.

Lastly, some acknowledgments with the deepest gratitude to:

- My wife, Angela, for her never ending love and untold sacrifices to support my work in the Social Justice Mission.
- Our children and their families for their love and interest in my activities.
- Father Pete [6] and Father John[7] for seventeen years of spiritual, pastoral and practical guidance, support and friendship.
- Father George [8] and his brother Montfort Fathers for providing their hospitality in a quiet space to pray, to reflect, to write.
- Our daughter, Susan, who found the time to word process the first draft of this testimony as she carried out her responsibilities as wife and mother of four young children.
- Our grandchildren Lawrence and Donna and their mother Carol who undertook the assignment to place the final draft on a computer disc.
- Harry Anderson for his professional assistance in editing.
- Kathleen Vetter for her professional and technical assistance with the final touches to be ready for publishing.
- Everyone who will develop their own testimony to social justice as a true disciple of Jesus Christ.

Bill McNamara

....

6 Monsignor Peter A. Chiara, Pastor Emeritus, St. Mary's Parish, East Islip, New York

7 Monsignor John D. Gilmartin, Former Director of Catholic Charities, Diocese of Rockville Centre, now, Pastor of St. Anne's Parish, Garden City, New York

8 Reverend George Werner, Superior, Montfort Spiritual Center, Bay Shore, New York

CHAPTER 1

IDENTITY

Who do people say that the son of man is?
Matthew 16:13

It is January 10, 1999 and I am returning from Washington D.C. on the twelve o'clock shuttle to MacArthur Airport. I have finished the snack luncheon when Jesus asks me, "Who do people say that I am"?

Jesus, may I begin to answer your question with a story. One morning there was an experience at the Eucharist in St. Mary's Church in Manhasset that is appropriate to the theme of this opening testimony. It was a weekday Mass in the late sixties, not long after the closure of the Second Vatican Council. There may have been eighteen to twenty people in the church. The incident is about one of the externals that came out of the Council, namely, the kiss of peace, more adequately defined as the "handshake" after the Our Father. I leaned over two pews to shake the hand of a bewildered elderly man. I was certain that he didn't have a clue what this was all about. When the Mass was over and we were together in the aisle making our exits, he expressed his puzzlement with the question:

Do I know you?

Jesus comments, perhaps with a little more penetration of what could be a prophetic question, "Do you really know the love, or the lack of it, of your brothers and sisters-locally, nationally, and globally"?

Jesus, not really. I think it is important to start with an inventory of where we are at as we look over the horizon into the next century.

The tone and content of the next two questions indicate Jesus wants action and not just a report as He asks "Where did you go wrong? Where do you go from here"?

Jesus you are asking the earlier question again after two thousand years have passed. You asked it then of your disciples. Their response identified the prophets.

Then there was the follow up. "But who do you say that I am"?[9]

Simon Peter said in reply "You are the Messiah, the Son of the Living God".[10]

You went on to affirm Peter that this Truth had been revealed to Him by Your heavenly Father and that Peter would be the rock upon which you will build your church.

Jesus replies, "The church is not the building of bricks and mortar. It is the people in community under the guidance of Peter and later his successors from whom will come the solid foundation for the future."

Yes, Jesus, may we always remember both points that you make.

Moving on Jesus asks, "Today I repeat the same questions. In the world—who do they say that I am? In the church—who do they say that I am? Bill—who do you say that I am"?

Jesus, with a sense of shame and deep sorrow, it seems as though much of the world doesn't seem to know You. The gap between rich and poor widens. Jesus, you walked thousands of miles from your hometown to the scattered cities, villages, and towns, including Jerusalem the religious and political center of your time. You

....

9 Matthew 16:15-16
10 Matthew 16:17

saw the homeless, the hurting, and the harassed. You always stopped. You healed. In the parable of the Good Samaritan you taught us to stop, to care, to heal. Today the homeless sleep on the sidewalks in the shadow of churches and government buildings, in the Jerusalems of our day. Their only source of heat in the winter comes from the escaping steam of a utility vent. The world, like the Levite and Priest, busily circle around the man or woman; homelessness has no gender lines, as they hurry on to their business, social, or religious activity.

"Maybe they have not heard the story of the Good Samaritan. Do not be too hard on them. You know that I love you all. Go on", Jesus replies as the radiant countenance of his face reflects his words.

Jesus unfortunately it seems that your beloved poor are the victims when many of our hospitals, Catholic included, seem to place a priority on the bottom line, or at best, they engage in token care for a few while the many are closed out. Medicine has made tremendous advances in technology while the economics of medical care are in shambles. Over forty million of your brothers and sisters are without access to adequate medical care. Jesus, how do I bring the challenge of Cardinal Bernadin, who is with you at this very moment, to this world? His statement before he died, that health care is not a commodity, should be a subject of serious reflection for everyone involved in the care of the sick or in distributing the insurance funds that provide financial support.

Jesus, so many of our youth don't seem to know who you are. This is evidenced from the ignorance of your presence in the Eucharist, to the disturbing number of suicides among them. In one of our parish communities on the eastern end of the island, there were five in one year.

Jesus strengthens me: "You have nothing to fear, but go on and tell me more".

Jesus, you suffered so much for the world's transgressions two thousand years ago. You suffer so much now where your Love has been countered by ignorance, indifference, or immobility. Maybe we should stop this conversation. No. We must go on. You know how your beloved disciple and teacher, John XXIII, evaluated the conditions around the world prior to the convening of the Council. "Unhappy and fatal decisions within and without, dissension, spiritual and moral decadence, and the ruin of nations sunk in error and in the grip of Satan." This was John XXIII's answer to your question.

Jesus says, "Go on, Bill."

On one recent Sunday, one thousand of the Catholic faithful gathered in the Cathedral in Baghdad to share your most sacred Body and Blood in the Eucharist while several hundred miles away in the Persian Gulf, the naval vessels of the United States and Great Britain rest and retool for another strike against the same city, perhaps only a few hundred yards from the Cathedral itself. The timing of this testimony coincided with back to back television coverage of the impeachment of a President, and the bombing of Baghdad. Oh, Jesus, why can't we sit down at the same table, respect our differences and resolve our problems. Maybe, Jesus, it is because we keep you away from the table.

When I roll the clock back to my own days in the Marine Corps, as a pilot, the experience included strafing, dropping bombs, and firing rockets on designated military targets, but not without the risk of killing the innocent. I saw a crew of seven burn up when they miscalculated a runway at one a. m. during a violent tropical storm. I made it back safely; they didn't. Then there was the time in the Philippines when I visited a field hospital. One of our planes had come down over Davao. The surviving crew members were fighting for their lives. We could only see the eyes of Major Bob, as his entire burned body was mummy-like covered with bandages.

When I recall the anxiety of counting the drone of the engines on the planes returning from a bombing mission, it is difficult to reconcile the seriousness of "Did they all return safely" with a bit of levity. But that kind of balance was necessary to maintain some degree of sanity. Thank you, Jesus, for always being there as a co-pilot. It was December 24, 1944 when all the planes returned safely from a mission over Rabaul. Since the next day was Christmas, the commanding officer declared a moratorium on any air strikes. The news was celebrated with a gathering at an improvised clubhouse, and by some over indulgence in the spirits by a few, led by the British trained executive officer, to the point where one half of the pilots were unable to meet the eight a. m. muster at the flight line on Christmas Day. The telephone rang that morning about eleven a. m. with a query from the exec that went something like this:

Duty Officer: "Flight Line, Lt. Downs."

Executive Officer: "Fagan here, what's going on, Red"?

Duty Officer: "Nothing much, Major, nothing much. Oh, by the way, the Colonel has scheduled a field march for twelve noon for all the pilots who missed the eight a. m. muster."

Executive Officer: "Bloody good show, bloody good show. Who is leading it"?

Duty Officer: "You are sir."

Well, in one hundred and twenty five degree heat the colonel led a three-hour march for the pilots who had failed to report to the muster. I watched as they carried their unpacked and rarely used back packs and rifles.

Where does this all fit into our social justice testimony? In our efforts to implement your justice teachings, Jesus, maybe I need a little more of the

- dedication of the commanding officer to the mission
- discipline in my prayer life to be faithful to the mission
- devotion to you, Jesus, as my copilot fifty-five years later as I strive to implement your mission
- development of a deep sense of and commitment to justice as an important component of being one of your disciples, in myself, in the church, and in the world that would truly answer your question, "Who do they say I am"? Yes, the leaders say it was a 'just' war. Sometimes I wonder. Was there another way earlier, before Pearl Harbor, that could have prevented the massive killings on both sides? What have we learned from it all Jesus?

"Not very much," Jesus replies with an obvious repulsiveness for war and its consequences.

Jesus, your concern for family life is so valid. The divorces in the Catholic and non-Catholic world have reached a staggering level. Domestic violence is rampant though not always visible. In the military alone there are long standing records of up to fifty thousand reported cases.

Last Christmas Day I met a bright, personable, courteous ten year-old boy. After an exchange of a few normal Christmas pleasantries, that did not include "Happy Holiday", I asked him where Christmas dinner would be enjoyed, with his parents or with his grandparents? He replied tragically, "I am going to my father's home. My mother will have her dinner at my grandmother's." The single parent syndrome once again.

Jesus, family life is so important. And then, Jesus, there is the subject of LIFE and the total lack of respect for it demonstrated in so many negative ways:

- Millions interfere with the hands of the Creator, while political leaders publicly express support for the teachings of your Church as a personal position, while legislatively, they fail to hear the cries of your infants in the womb.
- Others clamor for the extinction of the elderly or disabled who no longer can produce for society.
- And still others want an eye for an eye and a tooth for a tooth as they cry out for vengeance on death row inmates.

"Remember how when I was on earth I told the people to come to me when they were burdened and I would refresh them"? Jesus reminds me, "Please tell me more of your experiences."

There is a story that I would like to share with you, Jesus, that reflects another problem. This incident involved two ladies and myself at the end of a long workday. One lady could not release her car's emergency brake and sought my help. But before that was possible, the car backed up driverless and began a rotation around the rectangular parking lot at thirty five miles an hour. I called 911 and three police cars arrived within minutes of each other. The first officer with his hands on his hips remarked, "I never saw anything like this before". The second officer arrived on the scene and hands on hips exclaimed; "I never saw anything like this before." Then a sergeant arrived on the scene. The car by now was in its eighth or ninth rotation. Putting his seniority and expertise to work, after five tries he successfully launched a spare tire under the runaway car. This slowed the car down to a point where he could get behind the wheel and bring the car to a stop. What lesson can I learn from this story? Well, Jesus, our world is living the same kind of runaway pace, going round and round leaving little time for rest, relaxation, or for You. Worse still, Jesus, we have drawn our children into the same patterns as the adults. Our children need more time away from parental and societal pressure and more time to do things children should do.

Jesus replies with the never ending invitation, "Let the children come to me. Don't keep them so busy that they don't know me. But go on. Tell me more."

Well, Jesus, I don't think the adult world knows how much you love children. If they did, they would heed the message of one of your Baptist ministers on a recent Martin Luther King Day. He spoke of how every year, twenty-one percent of Rwanda's children die of hunger. Nightly news broadcasts show bloated stomachs and children's bodies covered with black flies. It is reported that a year ago the count was up to five hundred thousand when our President visited this war torn country. To this date no promised action has taken place, the minister stated. There must be other priorities! In 1986, your bishops tried to get us on the right track, but a mental lynching was led in opposition by many individuals of the corporate community of whom many were Catholics.[11]

....

11 Pastoral Letter of the United States Bishops, Economic Justice For All: Catholic Social Teaching and the U.S. Economy, 1986

The bishops reminded us that the economy exists to serve the people, not the other way around. How well you witnessed this by your own teachings and action. The bishops reminded us at the time:

- that economic life should be shaped by moral principles and ethical norms.
- that economic choices should be measured by whether they enhance or threaten human life, human dignity, and human rights.
- that a fundamental concern must be support for the family and the well being of children.
- and lastly, Jesus, your twentieth century bishops stated that the moral measure of any economy, here or abroad, is how the weakest are faring. Jesus, as you well know it is now a case where here in the United States there seems to be three nations geographically living side by side on the planet that our Father created.
- one nation that is prospering in a new information age, coping well with new economic challenges.
- a second nation is squeezed by declining real incomes and global economic competition. Our brothers and sisters worry about their jobs, health insurance, and affordable education for their children.
- and then, Jesus, there is a community growing more discouraged and despairing. Many of your children, our children, are on the bottom rung of the economic ladder, desperately poor in the richest nation on earth. Their parent's go from day to day in constant fear of losing the basic necessities of life.

Jesus, what should we do?

Jesus replies, "You know that I am very aware of all of this, but I am so happy that you share my sufferings with me. So go on and tell me more about the world's problems."

As a society, we try to celebrate your birthday in a world that has taken your name out of the Christmas greeting.

Jesus says, "And what happens the other three hundred and sixty four days of the year? Where was everybody when in the bitter cold of winter I slept on the sidewalk outside your parish church? But please, go on. Share your other concerns with me."

I would ask what has happened to the labor movement that once protected our brothers and sisters from exploitation. Has it lost pace with its mission of social justice? Is it just another corporate or political entity ignoring the welfare of the members?

Jesus, I hope this is not too long winded as some say I have a tendency to be.

Jesus replies, "You call them as you see them."

Finally, I must touch on the political climate.

Jesus comments as we pass over the county seat in Mineola, "Please do. As you well know I had experience with the political leaders of Rome and Israel when I was on earth."

Well, Jesus, you know there is a terrible apathy when it comes to voting. To begin with, people do not understand the Judeo/Christian Social Justice values. Unless they have a self-interest in an issue they do not seem to vote. Sometimes an election will have a low turnout of twenty to thirty percent, rarely higher. It is also a fact that the active voting groups are often influenced by the modern day spin doctors with negative broadcasting. Their influence is not only national but international.

Jesus lights a spark, "But don't they realize what a potential they have, a great gift from the Father, to address issues in the light of my teachings, to be a voice for change"?

Your message on justice is not being heard. Too often people are involved in only one issue to the exclusion of many other important issues that are concerned with life.

Jesus responds with a new insight, "Tell them to go out to the poor or the poor may come to them in unpleasant ways. How can they love the poor as I have commanded if they don't know what hurts them"?

Maybe, Jesus, society is too caught up in the fast moving world of technology with cellular phones, computers, recorders, stretch limousines, and luxury automobiles outclassing one another. We have lost the great gift of mutual presence.

"Remember, Bill, technology is all right as long as it never becomes a priority over me. Is that what has happened?

Go on, tell me a little about my Church in the middle of all of these concerns that worry both of us. Who do they say I am"?

Well, Jesus, certainly the Pope is bringing your justice message all over the world. He is articulate. He is visible. Social justice is finding a place on the Bishops' agenda. They are publishing pastoral letters on the subject. But it is like an umbrella. The cover is the Pope and the Bishops. But when you go under the cover to the supporting frame which is the pastors, priests, deacons, religious, and laity there is very little activity specifically targeted at social justice.

"Why"? Jesus asks.

That is a good question, Jesus. Some of it is based in fear. We hear preachers being cautioned, "Don't shake the congregation up" or "There are no poor in the community." Maybe we are afraid the Sunday collection will go down. I really don't know why there should be attendance fears. Only twenty to twenty five percent of the Catholics are in regular attendance anyway. The other denominations are having the same experience. There is also a tremendous void in education and training on social justice. How can we expect people to live in witness of your teachings if they do not hear the message? Frankly, those in the corporate world serving on boards, and on councils, together with the other lay leaders and in concert with the clergy, should be continually searching for the answer to these questions. If it were a business and they were only capturing twenty to twenty five percent of the customers, the "why" would become a priority.

In confidence Jesus responds, "Remember my promise. The gates of hell will not prevail over the rock of Peter upon which I built my church".

Maybe the church was in need of purgation and when it is over it will be much stronger.

Jesus, there are also other problems.

"Yes, how well I know. There are times that I recognize our church seems to have come a long way from Galilee. Go on."

Well, Jesus, we have to take a hard look inside the inner circle, the twenty to twenty five percent of active Catholics, before we go out to those who are hungry and searching. The early Christians inspired the rest of their communities by the way they loved one another. In our time, Divine Love cannot be experienced with one another if we have anyone in the inner circle of clergy, religious, or laity;

- who identifies a social justice homily as too political?
- who engages in gossip that breaks down the sacredness of the mission?
- who will invite and listen to only one point of view?
- who by words or actions will deliberately hurt, sometimes wound, another, be it bishop, pastor, priest, deacon, religious, or lay person. What happens to the peace of the Sunday Eucharist on the other six days? What happens to the Sunday gospel message on the other six days? I pray for the poor on Sunday but do I go out and touch their pain the rest of the week?
- who may be influenced too much by the voices of the well meaning corporate world at the expense of justice inside the Church structure as well as outside?

If we cannot live lovingly within the inner circle-within the twenty to twenty five percent of the active faithful, how can we possibly be recognized and inspire those who are outside?

We have to be more serious in our efforts to reach out to the seventy five to eighty percent of the Catholics who have left us after Baptism, after the first reception of your Body and Blood, and after the revisit of your Holy Spirit at Confirmation. An absence that exists until marriage. After marriage so many slip back into the seventy five to eighty percent and wonder why the vows don't hold.

You know, Jesus, I am beginning to wonder if I am too cynical, too negative. There are so many good things that are experienced by so many who have a close relationship with you.

Jesus replies, "Yes, I experience those relationships and I love those people very much. But I also love equally all the brothers and sisters who have wandered away. They are the lost sheep I spoke about when I was on earth. I want you to help in anyway you can. Don't worry about being too cynical or too negative. Your motive is to build the kingdom on earth. As long as you keep your entire focus on that effort I will be with you. I like your frankness. So go on. Are there other matters about the Church and who they say that I am? People should know who I am by the way they witness and live my gospel teachings. I came to serve, not to be served. My church has to be a Servant Church. If all of your concerns about cynicism or negativism result in hiding the truth about what stands in the way of bringing souls to live my lifestyle, then it is not my will. So please continue to bring your thoughts out in the open. You will all be so spiritually enriched by doing so."

Thank you, Jesus. I needed that encouragement. Frankly, I am bothered many times by the bureaucratic, institutional flavor of the Church: parish, diocese, and Rome. Does the burden of paperwork, programs upon programs, distract the clerical leadership from the mission of justice leading to evangelization? Will we ever have solidarity with the poor as long as our buildings, our dress, our lifestyles reflect the secular world, not the Servant Church? Will we ever have solidarity with the poor if we build large bank accounts with money that was contributed with the sole purpose of assisting the poor now, not some time in the maybe distant future. As one pastor recently stated: "If we are serious about being the Church of the poor, we have to first examine our own lifestyles, starting with rectory living."

"Do you have any thoughts as to why some members of your own family or young adults of other families are searching for another parish or a church of a different persuasion"? Jesus asks with an expression of deep concern.

You are centering on the main purpose of this testimony. Jesus, the present structure is not working for a substantial number of individuals. We lost you as our focus. Where do we go from here? We should choose you as the model for our lifestyle. You came from the Father. In our midst you taught us how to pray. You taught us how to act. You spent most of your public life with the marginalized, the sick, the oppressed, and the broken. You healed them. You also confronted the authorities whenever there was injustice. You didn't pull any punches. In the world, the answer to your continuing question, "Who do they say that I am"? rests in following you by living the way you lived. In the Church, the answer to this same question, "Who do they say that I am"?, rests in the same answer in following you by living the way you lived. Lastly, really first, for it must start with me, when you ask me "Who do you say that I am"? the answer rests in my commitment to follow you in a lifestyle that reflects your lifestyle. This was a message of the second Vatican council that we missed.

Jesus replies with a question that has prophetic overtones, "Bill, do you think when this begins to happen in a substantial way that attendance at religious services will come back, that vocation to ordained ministries will increase, and with new inspired leadership, the Catholic Church will be truly a Servant Church with everyone sharing their gifts? Do you think then that will be an attraction to the separated members from My Body"?

Yes, Jesus. The challenge is to move our vision of church from a building of bricks and mortar to a movement of the grace of the Sunday liturgies and sacraments within that building out to the community on Monday through Saturday. This is the message that has to be heard over and over again. That was good timing as the wheels just touched down on the runway here at MacArthur Airport.

As we taxi in to the terminal, Jesus asks: "Bill, can an executive of a company manufacturing computers in the twenty-first century live just as I lived"?

1 John 2:5-6

CHAPTER 2

OLD WINE

Why do you call me, Lord, Lord, but not do what I command? I will show you what someone is like who comes to me, listens to my words and acts on them. That one is like a person building a house, who dug deeply and laid the foundation on rock; when the flood came, the river burst against that house but could not shake it because it had been well built. But the one who listens and does not act is like a person who built a house on sand. When the river burst against it, it collapsed at once and was completely destroyed.

Luke 6: 46-49

It is now early the following the morning as Jesus begins with a question that displays his interest in me. "The Father has blessed you with a large part of almost a century of experience in family, work and church. Tell me what life in my Church was like to you during those years."

Well, Jesus, I have to separate the first forty six years from the past thirty four.

"Why"? Jesus asks.

The Second Vatican Council changed my life. As a matter of fact, as I reflect on both periods, I feel somehow I was cheated out of something very rich and beautiful during those pre-Vatican Council years. The call from you was to develop our relationship, to listen to you and most importantly to translate your words into action. I never heard your call in the earlier years. It was different. If not, why the Council? John XXIII knew that the Church was off course and the navigational instruments had to be retooled and directed towards a renewed Beacon of Light.

"Tell me, Bill, what you remember about those earlier years." Jesus asks.

It will only be with your help that this aged mind will be capable of the recollection you request. Jesus, let me try to bring some kind of order to your question that makes some sense. We are all here as a result of circumstances that are beyond our control. In 1898 my mother as a young teenager left her home in Ireland to sail over the Atlantic Ocean to the United States. She left her family and home because there was not enough food on the table to feed her parents and six siblings. Yet the house probably provided more comfort than the cramped conditions on the ship well below the water line. Many times she would recall her feelings and emotions as the ship pulled away from the dock. The immediate desire to be back with the family without food was nestled in the pit of her stomach. She would further recall that if she had the ability to swim she would have jumped overboard and gone back home. So, Jesus, had she been able to swim, this testimony would not be taking place.

"Go on, tell me about the earliest years." Jesus requests.

Well, my birthplace was Boston where your Church has deep roots, one of the largest Catholic dioceses in the United States. I am sure, Jesus, that you are interested in baseball, for your Love has no boundaries. My birth came in the year that the Boston Red Sox last won the World Series, 1918. With a smile, Jesus comments, "That must be a long time for you Bill."

The world was engulfed in a bloody experience, World War I, the war that was to end all wars. But was it not really only the beginning of more violence and killing throughout the century? Jesus, why don't we come to You, listen to your words and act on them? In 1918 there were no answers to curb and cure the epidemics of influenza and polio. Both illnesses were experiencing heavy death tolls. The city of Boston was an attraction for a better way of life to thousands of people of Irish and Italian descent. However, as you know Jesus, they struggled for survival in a society that was controlled by Protestants. The unwelcoming climate was "No Catholics Need Apply". This is not all new to your Church. The pages of the history of the Church in New York, Boston, and other parts of the northeast corner of the United States are filled with the supporting activities of agencies like Catholic Charities, other societies and the parish schools that welcomed the newcomers. They assisted them materially to positions of self-sufficiency and citizenship. At some times your Church seemed to be standing alone. Yet, your voice cried out for the racial and economic equality. Hospitals were built and staffed by nuns to respond to the medical needs of the poor, including immigrants. Orphanages were built to provide a home for homeless children. How well I remember once a year after each Mass on a Sunday when the orphans would stand in line by age at the rear of the church waiting anxiously for the couple that would be willing to take them home assuming the role of their adopted parents. Sometimes, Jesus, when I become involved and speak out for the immigrants it is interpreted as something new in the life of the Church.

In those earlier years baptisms were scheduled with an urgency, one week after birth, out of fear that if the infant died he/she would end up in a nothing place called Limbo. My mother was a victim of influenza and unable to attend the baptism. Obviously, baptism meant nothing to me at that point in time. Later on there was the explanation that baptism was the removal of the black spot on the white cloth. Then there was churching when the mother, now well enough to travel outside the home, went to the church building, and at the altar she held a candle and received a blessing from the priest. To this day I am not sure what it was all about.

Jesus reminds me, "Didn't you forget to mention your own illness"?

I did. You are referring to the bout with polio when I was one year old. It was a mild case in comparison to the sufferings and deaths of so many of my peers. Deo Gratias. Then followed eight years of education, after one year in the public school kindergarten, in the parish school staffed by the dedicated Sisters of Notre Dame de Namur. I add to this several years as an altar boy, no girls at that time. Confirmation was in the eighth grade at the age of twelve. What is tucked away in my memory about this event? It was fear of a question about doctrine from the Bishop or a slap on the face, but the joy of some ice cream and cake was its joyful conclusion.

"Bill, tell me about your parents." Jesus inquires with his continuing interest.

My public high school days saw the death of my father who was a Boston fireman, shortly after my sixteenth birthday. One of my memories is a snapshot of him driving a boiler apparatus with the bellies of the horses close to the pavement of the street as they responded to a burning house. My parents saw to it that my religious education continued throughout the public high school years, one hour a week in the lower church. My father was a great provider even on a most modest salary of forty dollars a week. But not without periods of alcoholic depression in the economic struggle. His death left us with nothing except a heavily mortgaged house. How often a bank officer would call looking for overdue payments as my mother struggled with extremely limited resources to meet the payment schedules. My father's visions of this son graduating from Harvard and also becoming an accomplished violinist were gone. The need for repeating a grade and attending one summer school probably had blurred that vision in prior years. That pattern was probably a test from you, Jesus, as to where the rest of this life would go.

Jesus assures me, "I knew that you would be okay. Go on with the story about your parents."

My father left a legacy never to be forgotten. On Saturday mornings we would travel by trolley for five-cents to the downtown market, where we would buy the meat and poultry for the coming week at discount prices. Frequently, we would pass a disabled man or woman reaching out with their hand, begging. My father would always reach into very limited resources and give the person a coin and then as we moved on he would turn to me and say, "Never pass a beggar."

This is the story of the Good Samaritan—vintage of 1930. This is a legacy which lives on within me to the present day. Jesus, maybe this was the first time you spoke to me and I didn't recognize you.

"Yes, Bill, I was planting a seed. Your father was my instrument. That lesson was more important to you than a summer school of Greek."

Jesus, you know how devoted my mother was to your Blessed Mother. She probably never missed a day without saying the rosary until she was past ninety and very ill. During those days I would try to say it for her in the nursing home. Speaking of her illness, for five years, Angela, my wife, took care of her, day and night. Jesus, you must chuckle on occasion when you witness the superstitions of some cultures. During a thunderstorm my mother would draw all the shades and proceed to sprinkle holy water throughout the house including the closets, a custom she carried from her Irish home. I will take a few more minutes to round out the picture of the Mc Namaras in those early pre Vatican days. I had a sister who died in infancy. My brother, eight years older, had completed his professional training as a funeral director and struggled in a depressed economy to establish a business. My financial contribution to the household came in the form of a part time job after school and Saturdays in a grocery store. After graduation from high school, it was a full time job, running the street, as it was called, delivering stocks and bonds in the financial district. The depression brought about a salary cut from twelve dollars a week to a take home pay of ten dollars and seventy six cents. There was a contribution of twenty-four cents from the gross of eleven dollars to support Social Security and Unemployment Compensation. This was the beginning of the social agenda of President Roosevelt. If I roll the clock back out of this present age of cellular phones, computers and faxes to the twenties we find the era of crystal radios. Then, in the thirties we had the advanced tube radio that carried the voice of the controversial Father Coughlin and his social justice agenda, which met strong opposition. Some things never change.

"What about your experience with religion? What about spirituality? What about your relationship with me"? Jesus asks as he hits a vital nerve.

Good question Jesus. As a pre Vatican Council Catholic, I never gave much thought to what religion was beyond obedience to a set of rules and regulations and my fear of breaking them. I seem to have been more focused on negative commissions than positive omissions and there were times when a calculator would have been helpful. To make it perhaps a little clearer, the sinful acts of what a person shouldn't do versus the sinful act of not doing what one is called to do in charity and in justice towards a hurting brother or sister. I never got into the sins of omission. It was a religion that seemed to be permeated by fear, fire, brimstone and hell. As my former pastor describes it "Obedience to the Ten Commandments makes one a good Jew, not necessarily a good Christian, a good Catholic." This is the same pastor who in the early eighties publicly declared that the Church was dead as he sought to bring the vitality and the energy of the Second Vatican Council to his parish community. It was an era when the emphasis seemed to be on sin and punishment, not mercy and love. Somehow, I missed the true impact of your commandment, Jesus—to love your God with your whole heart, your whole soul and your neighbor as yourself. It was a religion where individualism was in control; saving one's soul was the goal. One attained this goal by:

- private prayers, very mechanical
- indulgences which were abundant as a built in promise with every prayerful effort
- quantity which was more important than quality
- more and more prayers with a higher and higher reward and the resultant closeness to God in Heaven

As to spirituality I was not aware of such a thing. It was not in my vocabulary. Certainly a spirituality that melded the Trinitarian Divine love of the Father—you Jesus—the Holy Spirit—into a circular oneness with one's self and neighbor. I didn't even have a clear picture of who was the neighbor. As to my relationship with you, Jesus, if someone even suggested such a thought I would have considered it to be blasphemy.

Jesus continues to nudge, "What do you remember about liturgies, the sacraments? You spoke earlier about Baptism and Confirmation. What about the others? What about vocations"?

Well, Jesus, as you know Sunday Mass was compulsory under the fear of mortal sin if you missed it. Speaking of missing, one had to be present for the three principal parts, which were the Offertory, Consecration and Communion. We were required to fast from midnight until the reception of your Body. The Mass was in Latin so most of the congregation did not understand the words unless they carried a missal. We had High Masses with three priests—a celebrant, a deacon and a sub deacon. Was this kind of a class distinction within the ordained priesthood? On All Soul's Day, November 2nd, a priest would celebrate three Masses back to back, wearing black vestments. The black was carried over into all funeral Masses. What a sad message versus white in celebration of the departed being close to you, Jesus, as you promised.

Jesus seems pleased. "I am happy that you remember my promise to the apostles at my last meal with them when I told them I was going to prepare a place for them and I would come back and take them to myself.[12] Certainly this is no occasion for mourning in black."

We used incense frequently at Holy Hours, Benedictions and Eucharistic Liturgies to honor your Presence. We don't do that very often now. You know Jesus, I miss that sacredness. Another pre-Vatican council practice was that we were forbidden to eat

....

12 John 14:2-3

meat on Friday. Of course, Jesus, there was nothing sinful about eating a two-pound lobster. On Holy Thursday thousands of your faithful would travel around the diocese to visit a required number of seven churches and as a reward be assured a place in Heaven.

During the high school years, I attended religion classes in the lower church of the parish that held six hundred. The upper church seated one thousand and often there were two simultaneous Masses with standing room only. What has happened? Then there were those who by choice stayed close to the door, some things never change. Confessions were frequent. The confession was always in darkness. Was that somehow to hide the shame or lighten the guilt? Yet, has the pendulum swung too far in the opposite direction when one can witness two priests waiting for one hour without a single penitent? Yes, Jesus, you asked about vocations. As for me, like many young men, there was the question of the validity of a call to the priesthood but the scholastic record in Greek and the financial needs at home took care of that consideration. Vocations were plentiful with some candidates entering junior seminaries as early as a high school freshman. How well I remember the long processions of seminarians, two hundred strong, two abreast with their flowing black capes and birettas as they passed my home two days a week in this disciplined time of exercise. At the same time there was another group of two hundred going in a different direction.

Jesus looks off into space as he says; "You should never forget the dedication of the priests of those days as they followed Me in administering the sacraments to the faithful. I haven't forgotten them. Many of them are with me at this very moment. Go on now. Give me some impressions of the life in the Church, incidents, and things you remember. They don't have to always be inspiring."

Well, Jesus, one thing that comes to mind during my grade school years was seeing the Cardinal Archbishop traveling around the diocese in a Rolls Royce, driven by a double breasted blue serge uniformed Japanese chauffeur with a large, standard black poodle sitting proudly erect on the rear seat at the side of the

Cardinal. It was a time when the Cardinal Archbishop of New York asked Dorothy Day to remove the word "Catholic" from the *Catholic Worker* publication because her work and words with and about the poor might be misunderstood or threatening to the comfort of the society of those days.

Jesus observes, "Isn't it interesting Bill that through My grace, the mission of Dorothy Day lives on in the work and the publications. Sorry to interrupt your memory probing. Go on please."

It was a point in time when at an annual fund raising dinner event for the Cardinal, one thousand men in black ties sat at tables on the main floor of Symphony Hall while the women were restricted to the balcony.

"Go on Bill. This is very interesting."

Jesus, You taught and prayed for our Oneness and yet in those days we were forbidden to participate with or enter into a Protestant Church, be it a prayer service or a Boy Scout meeting. We were forbidden to read the Bible. This was an example of fear or concern that I would misinterpret the meanings. Any sense of what the Trinity was all about was left to the minds of the theologians. Lay people couldn't handle mystery—even in faith? I should close these words about Church with the statement that religion was a very private affair. Your name might slip off the tongue in a curse, probably too often, but never in a positive, public proclamation of the "Good News." Thank you Jesus, for changing all that through your inspiration in the documents of the Second Vatican Council.

Jesus asks, "What about our poor? How did they connect with life in our church? Were they in solidarity with those who were blessed with and enjoyed more of the world's material goods?"

Well, Jesus, you are leading me into the main thrust of this testimony. In charity, then and now, we are a very generous people, be it a financial response to a visiting missionary, or a hurricane in Florida or Central America, or an earthquake in South America, we always have and I am sure we will respond abundantly in the future. My own patterns of charity were paralleled pretty much as a way of life by my peers. Namely, a coin or two in the St. Vincent de Paul poor box, a turkey at Thanksgiving and a few toys at Christmas to some poor family seemed to satisfy the charity obligation avoiding any possible guilt trip.

Jesus asks, "Isn't that good"?

Yes, Jesus, it is. The problem then and now is justice. Distributive justice was not addressed then and as a matter of fact it is very low on the agenda of your brothers and sisters at the present time. What did exist then and is very high on the present agenda is commutative justice, not of the heart but of the mind. They should get what they deserve, an eye for an eye, a tooth for a tooth. This climate heavily outweighs the scales of mercy and love, Your Mercy, Your Love. Justice that addresses the causes and strives for a correction was not present then nor for the most part even now.

Discrimination and brutality were not foreign to the culture of those days. In my early years how well I remember the sight of a thirty year old son of Irish Catholic parents, laying on the blood covered floor of the paddy wagon, a police van. He was an alcoholic who in an intoxicated state tried to resist arrest. This was justice! In my early years in the department store business I recall a customer who, dissatisfied with the decision of a manager who refused a refund on a clock that had been abused, threatened me for supporting the decision with, "I'll smash this clock in your face, you Jew bastard." Sad, but indicative of the stereotypes and discrimination that existed then as well as now.

Even though Jesus had spent the entire night in prayer under the stars on a hill in Fort Salonga, He shows no signs of being tired. "We have so much yet to talk about. What do we have to do to build our Church as truly the Servant Church. Is there anything you wish to add about the pre-Second Vatican Council years"?

Yes, Jesus. I would like to mention some changes that I believe were significant as they were prompted by your Holy Spirit. One was to be as concerned with my spiritual well being as with my maintenance of Marine Corps physical fitness. This was in the early fifties and occurred in an early morning three-mile walk. The exact spot where I stepped off a curbstone is as clear in my mind as I speak, as it was then. What followed over a few years of those fifties was some spiritual reading, rosaries, that had more reflection on the mysteries, teaching religion to high school students and three years together with Angela, in formal study of theology with the Dominican Fathers at the Cardinal Cushing School for the Laity. Jesus, You inspired your brother, Richard, to be out a bit in front of the Council. Then came the Marian year, I think it was 1953, when Catholics were asked to make a commitment to participate in the Mass one weekday every week for the year. Now, Jesus, as I look back on this I realize what a great grace this was that you bestowed on me then and as it led to the past forty-six years of daily participation in the Eucharistic Liturgy. I am certain that this great source of spiritual nourishment has had a tremendous influence on what was to follow in my years as a post Vatican Council Catholic. It carried me through:

- the family responsibilities to a wife and eight children
- the work responsibilities from an executive trainee to executive management in the department store business
- the little earlier than norm (one year) for retirement to be an active participant in the Social Justice Mission of the Church
- the struggles of the ups and downs of the economy
- the illnesses and losses of loved ones.

Through it all, You were always there. Thank you, Jesus.

Jesus replies, "Bill, thank you."

Jesus, as I reflect on the period just prior to the convening of the Council, I realize how empty the life of the Church was in so many ways and how turbulent the world was at the same time. Thank you, Jesus, for sending John XXIII to lead us. I only pray that the memory of him will not slip off into oblivion but rather that he will be remembered for the rationale and inspiration for the convening of the Council. At the moment very few hear about him. Of course, it is almost forty years ago. Thank you for reminding me to be an instrument of this remembrance of him.

"Go back Bill to the signs of the times prior to the Council. What were you witnessing"?

Well Jesus, it was a time when the world was plunged into so many grave anxieties and troubles,

- the post World War II period
- our youth were very unsettled off campus and rioting on campus
- we had made a transition from "hot" wars to "cold" wars
- the threat (real or imagined) of annihilation lurked in the shadows of the free world
- new and peculiar behavioral patterns blossomed throughout society
- while almost everyone desired harmony and peace, yet, conflicts grew more acute and the threats multiplied.

It was in this global climate that Pope John XXIII, on January 20, 1959 after a long period of discernment and prayer, heard your questions, Jesus, that led to the convening of the Council.

"What should the Church be and do"?

"Should my Mystical Barque continue to drift along tossed this way and that by the ebb and the flow of the tides"?

"Instead of new warnings, should not my Church be a Beacon of Light"?

John XXIII responded with another question, "What could that exemplary light be? The world is starving for peace"?

Jesus, You guided the Pope; "If you return the Church to Me, the world will gain. I have been on the cross with my arms outstretched for two thousand years. Where have you got in proclaiming the Good News? How can you bring my authentic doctrine to your contemporaries"?

John XXIII, his frustration reflected, as he strove to answer the questions. However this inspired decision and dramatic announcement produced nothing in the way of an affirmative response from the seventeen Cardinals who heard it nor of the rest of the world and particularly the Catholic world. The Council was opposed by the Archbishop of New York as well as many others. On the ride back to his quarters he felt tired of everyone, of everything. This is a mood, that, like John XXIII, I feel on occasion when the fruits of the Council around justice seem to be so barren. Yet, it was not a matter of his personal feelings. John XXIII was embarked on the will of the Lord. He needed silence and recollection.

As you know, Jesus, in spite of the opposition, twenty two hundred bishops from all around the world gathered in Rome on October 11, 1962 and for two and a half years under the guidance of the Holy Spirit addressed the discernment and prayerful questions of John XXIII.

Jesus, I conclude these thoughts around the challenges of the Pre Vatican Council period and say Good Night.

"Bill, sleep on this question: Can a postal clerk live in the twenty first century just as I lived."

1 John 2: 5-6

CHAPTER 3

NEW WINE

I tell you most solemnly, whoever believes in Me will perform the same works as I do myself. He/she will perform even greater works because I am going to the Father. Whatever you ask for in My Name, I will do so that the Father may be glorified in the Son. If you ask for anything in my name I will do it.

John 14: 12-14

After a breakfast of fruit and cereal, we continue the conversation of last evening.

Jesus, what was it about the Second Vatican Council that seemed to take hold on me? As you know from day one, I was drawn to the progress of the Council in bits and pieces over two and a half years. To this day I read and re-read many of the Council documents, particularly the ones entitled *The Church—The Church in the Modern World* and *The Laity*. As I look back on the Pre Vatican period, somehow I feel that I was cheated out of the fullness, the richness of your life on earth, your prayer life, your teachings, your healings, your concern with injustice. Today, I am certain that I was being led by your Spirit. Maybe you wanted me to experience those earlier pre-council days as part of your plan, for to have lived those days gave me a deep appreciation of a commitment to another way. Today, I am certain that this was the most important happening in the Church in centuries and that you were calling me to be a part of it, as each one of your followers are being called to be active participants. I am being invited to fulfill the promise, Jesus, that you made at your Last Supper with the apostles. You will do the same works as I do myself. You will do even greater works.

Jesus reminds me, "I said to Philip at the Last Supper, 'Have I been with you for so long a time and you still don't know me?' Bill, didn't you know that I was there with you."

I'm afraid I didn't at the time. I believe that although I was being stirred a bit about the activities in Rome, at the same time, I was being influenced by other factors as they related to job, family and children's education. You well know how I changed my work from Boston to Long Island. Some of the children were not at home having moved on to their callings. Some were still in college, others in high school and one daughter in grammar school.

"Yes, I know you made that move. Do you remember anything else that may have given you a clue to my promise then or now"? Jesus asks.

Now that you ask that question I recall one Sunday in our new parish of St. Mary's in Manhasset how Father Weist, our pastor, announced that the parish was going to start a St. Vincent de Paul Conference to respond to the needs of the poor in the community. Frankly, I thought that he had lost contact with reality. Why, there couldn't be any poor in one of the richest communities in Long Island. Then I quickly came to the conclusion that the conference was being formed to respond to any needs that might come up on Spinney Hill which was a community of no more than two hundred black families.

Jesus comments, "It sounds to me as though Bill didn't have much of a handle on who were the poor."

It is interesting Jesus, that later on when I became involved in parish social ministry, I would hear from some pastors and Protestant ministers, "Oh, we don't have any poor in our parish." How well you know Jesus that I needed an education around an identification as to who are the poor that you once said we will always have with us. For now I am certain of your Presence back in Boston when I volunteered to be part of the St. Vincent de Paul mission even though it was for a short time. But it became the catalyst to volunteer again and say yes to Father Weist's invitation. Eight years as the conference president there in Manhasset together with three years as head of a conference in St. Mary's East Islip provided eleven years of more and more opportunities to not only know who the poor truly were but also to touch their pain. Somehow, I was able to find some space in my "I didn't have time" agenda without any effect on my family and work responsibilities.

"Was there any one incident that helped you gain some insight as to who are My poor"? Jesus asks, as He seems to be on a subject of real concern to him.

Yes, Jesus, and it came very soon after we formed the conference. The call came from a white mother with five children ages one to nine. Up to the day before our home visit she thought that she had a perfect marriage. Now, she was in an emotional state of shock to discover that the husband had deserted her and the children for another woman. He left her with no money, only a heavily mortgaged home which in those days was probably worth a quarter of a million dollars. Now, I am beginning to have a sense of who are your poor that you have called me to serve and how it reaches well beyond the society established boundaries of the stereotyped and minorities. Racial diversity in that North Shore community was small in comparison to what you will lead us to later on. The subject reminds me of the time I told my mother during a long distance call that one of our daughters had announced her engagement to be married.

"What's the boy's name"? she asked.

That time there were sons-in-law who were of Polish and Italian descent.

I told her his name was Cosimo Caltabiano. With that she said "William, aren't there any Americans on Long Island"? Had she forgotten the discrimination era of "No Catholics need apply." Did some of this subtle but never the less negative posture ever creep into her son's bones?

Jesus keeps the flow of the early years on Long Island moving along. “You know, Bill, that I often heard you tell people that I waved a carrot in front of you to bring you to the south shore of Long Island. Tell us how I did it.”

Jesus, I remember it so well. By 1979 most of the children were married and had left the house so I begin to think seriously about retirement three to four years into the future. Angela and I have decided on condominium living and we found a small beautiful community on the Great South Bay. When we drove in the gate “this was it.” Jesus, I didn’t know it at the time, but you were there with your carrot. You had a plan but I didn’t know it. I referred earlier to three years of Vincentian work at St. Mary’s parish in East Islip. When we moved there I had a desire to continue the St. Vincent de Paul mission but there was no conference. There was only one man responding to the needs of all the poor in that community. He was a good man but as you know, Jesus, I was later to find so much of the gatekeeper mentality in other parishes as well, too few trying to serve too many. It is key to this testimony. Well, after six months of fruitless conversations with the Vincentian and an associate pastor, I went to see the pastor. In fifteen minutes the pastor made a decision to expand the conference. At the first meeting of nine volunteers I was selected to be the president. In a short period of two years we grew to eighteen in number. After three years your spirit is working on me again, but I didn’t know it. I am experiencing a disturbing sense that there has to be something more to helping people in need than handing them a bag of food or paying a month’s rent. This helped individuals in a crisis, but we were not addressing the causes of injustice. We were not instruments, the server and the served, of change, of freeing individuals to be self sufficient.

Jesus asks, “Bill, how did you respond to this insight”?

Remember now that I have been following the Council teachings. I am being influenced as to how the people of God were being called to witness the gospel in the modern world. However, I needed something beyond my own self-study. You sent a new pastor, Monsignor Peter Chiara (Father Pete, as he prefers), who had just returned from six months sabbatical in Rome where he was updated with a study of the Second Vatican Council documents. Jesus, thank you, as this was ready made for where I was then. He arrived full of your Spirit. This is an awareness that I have now but probably didn't have then. Father Pete was filled with a vision of a new Church. It included addressing the implementation of many of what I like to call the externals of the Council. Some of them had already been initiated by the former pastor.

"What were they, Bill"?

Jesus, as I list them I am reminded how there are still a few "who long for the good old days."

- The altar was turned to face the people.
- The altar rails were removed.
- The Mass was changed from Latin to English.

We now have lay lectors, men and women, including some youth.

Then, there are men and women who are Eucharistic Ministers for the Mass as well as visits to the homebound.

Father Pete also addressed what I prefer to call the internals, which are the heart and soul of the Council. Jesus, how different it is from my experience in the Pre-Council years. There was a new understanding of Baptism, our call to share our gifts and talents with those in need. There was a new role for the laity and an exciting new role for women. Dialogues that included everyone were a key component of the vision. Father Pete brought a real sense of community in the social justice mission which was and is still all centered on you, Jesus, as our model. You have this great balance of communications with your Father through prayer and then out in your spirit of charity to heal the hurting, in the spirit of justice to confront the authorities on injustice. This all lit some sparks in me and I began to respond to Father Pete's suggestion that I go out and visit three parishes that had responded to the Council call and started what was then identified as Parish Outreach. One of your other priests, Monsignor John Gilmartin, (Father John as he prefers), had heard Your call and was a key player, first in a parish, later in Catholic Charities, in the social justice mission of Your Church. Jesus, between the conferences with Father Pete and three solid uninterrupted hours with Father John, you have me eating the carrots out of your Hands. I see the Church as all the people of God. I, too, have a vision of a new community built on your two greatest commandments of Love. For the first time since the early morning curbstone incident You speak to me again. You are so busy with all of us, do you remember?

Jesus reminds me of His presence at the time; "I do remember, Bill. You were returning to your pew in the Church at St. Mary's, East Islip, with the Eucharist when I prompted you to 'Give of yourself.' You heard me and soon after, retired, eighteen months before your sixty fifth birthday, and volunteered to start a parish outreach at your church."

Jesus, thank you for the call. Thank you for the grace to listen. Thank you for the grace to say YES. As Jesus withdraws to a private place for prayer to the Father, He leaves me with this question, "Bill, can a banking executive live in the twenty first century just as I live"?

1 John 2:5-6

CHAPTER 4

PAIN

While the crowd was pressing in on Jesus and listening to the Word of God, He was standing by the Lake of Gennesaret. He saw two boats there alongside the lake; the fishermen had disembarked and were washing their nets. Getting into one of the boats, the one belonging to Simon, He asked him to put out a short distance from the shore. Then He sat down and taught the crowds from the boat. After He had finished speaking, He said to Simon, "Put out into deep water and lower your nets for a catch." Simon said in reply, "Master, we have worked hard all night and have caught nothing, but at your command I will lower the nets." When they had done this, they caught a great number of fish and their nets were tearing. They signaled to their partners in the other boat to come to help them. They came and filled both boats so that they were in danger of sinking. When Simon Peter saw this, he fell at the knees of Jesus and said, "Depart from me Lord for I am a sinful man." For astonishment at the catch of fish they had made seized him and all those with him, and likewise James and John, the sons of Zebedee who were partners of Simon. "Do not be afraid; from now on you will be catching men." When they brought their boats to the shore, they left everything and followed Him.

Luke 5: 1-11

Jesus has just crossed over from one side of Lake Ronkonkoma to the shoreline. He encourages me to continue with the conversation of last evening. After reading Luke's testimony, I comment to Jesus, how well this gospel story has repeated itself over the past two centuries. How well it has repeated itself in my own experience. The elements of doubt, fear and commitment that were there then with Peter were present with me in 1982. Doubt, or maybe it was more anxiety, as to whether or not a large number of people in the community would come forward to serve and be served. Perhaps, it was a fear that we would be swallowed up economically. Finally, there was some concern around the faith commitment to leave the corporate world and follow you.

Jesus encourages me with a reminder from his teachings, "Do not worry." [13] How well you know, Jesus, that the doubt was soon dissipated as the mission of outreach became more and more visible throughout the community. I soon learned—doubt no longer—that there WERE poor in our community. Do you remember, Jesus, how year after year more and more of your brothers and sisters who were hurting in some kind of pain or brokenness came to your Church for help? The stereotype of who the poor were was destroyed. They were from different income levels, that is, low, middle, high and no income at all. When you were on earth, you welcomed everyone to your side. As your compassionate, caring Church became more and more visible throughout the community, they came: welfare recipients, sex offenders, unemployed, depressed, ill, elderly, prostitutes, runaways, homeless, pregnant teenagers, Catholics, non Catholics, Jewish, Agnostics, Atheists. Regardless of religious persuasion, they came. So often it was heard, "I didn't know the Church cared." Many times they came back to be part of the parish community, sometimes to serve others.

Jesus adds, "Oh, how that pleases me. They were coming to

....

13 Matthew 6:25-34

me through the Church for healing. But tell me, as more and more people came for help how were you able to provide the response to their needs"?

Testing the memory a bit, Jesus, it came from an ever increasing, continuous message about you as the model, about our baptismal call to share the gifts and talents that the Father has given us, to be a member of a Servant Church. As a result, doctors, dentists, lawyers, bankers, accountants, business people, teachers, nurses, trades people, housewives, retirees, government employees-women and men alike, young and old, came forward in answer to your call—to model you. They had the same anxieties, the same fears but thanks to you, the same commitment.

"You must have needed financial help. Where did that come from"? Jesus asks.

Now, this doesn't surprise you, I'm sure. It came from you. There are many wonderful people in all of our communities, but there are so many burdened with economic and family responsibilities that they are unable to share their gifts out in the community. They do not have the time yet they desire to be a part of your mission. Did you not inspire them to share some financial assistance with those in need? In a seven-year period the contributions rose in cadence with the needs. The amount was four thousand dollars in the first year, primarily from the poor box. In the last year the amount rose to one hundred and two thousand dollars. The donors ran from a widow's contribution of five dollars every month to the affluent executives' gifts of fifteen thousand and ten thousand dollars respectfully. This was money intended for assistance to the poor and it always flowed to the poor, never to build a bank account. Father Pete would not have it any other way. Jesus asks, "Did you ever worry, Bill, that you would not have the necessary funds to meet the needs of the poor"?

Well Jesus, I remember one Holy Thursday when we didn't have the funds to meet the rent needs of a single female parent with six mouths to feed. I had received a call from the rectory office. An anonymous person had left a bank check for ten thousand dollars with the explanation: "I see the great charitable works of your Parish Outreach but I am unable to give them some time so this is one way to help. I want this money to go out to those in need." On more than one occasion we would find ourselves with a zero bank balance and yet it always corrected itself. Within twenty—four hours we would be into the black through the love of some generous benefactor. I never had any doubts about your presence. The earlier doubt and fear were gone once and for all.

Jesus questions me, "Bill, I hear that some of my brothers and sisters doubt the validity of the stated needs that other brothers and sisters convey to you. Is there really a substantial amount of fraud"?

Jesus, I will answer your question this way. In my thirty-seven years in the department store business I had a reputation for being extremely liberal when it came to approval of refunds, partial credits and/or exchanges. I always felt that ninety-nine percent of the people who come back to a store for that purpose are sincere. In their heart they feel the store or the product has done them an injustice. I may not agree with them but with respect for their mindset the request would be granted by me. I felt that I didn't want to hurt the ninety-nine percent to protect us from the one percent who might have fraudulent motives. They will beat the system one way or another. I always felt the same way about the financial or material assistance to individuals seeking our help. If I stereotype, if I am on guard beyond reasonable assessments of the needs, I will hurt the ninety-nine percent and Jesus, is not the one percent the individual who causes more rejoicing in heaven than the ninety nine?

"Bill, do you think that the faithful twenty to twenty-five percent of Catholics who come to the Eucharist every Sunday see justice as an integral part of their Catholic life, as integral as the sacraments"?

I am afraid most of them don't, Jesus. Charity, yes. Justice based on Catholic social teachings, no.

"I like stories, Bill. Perhaps the people you are sharing your testimony with would be interested in some of the experiences you and the others serving had during that period."

Yes, Jesus. I agree. Statistics are okay for a general overview but one has to touch the pain as you did throughout your life on earth. I didn't say public life for I am sure it was always your lifestyle, in the unrecorded time before the reading of the scroll of Isaiah about the purpose of your mission. It is so much a part of the foundation of Judeo/Christian social justice values.

"Go on." Jesus prompts me again to continue with some stories.

One cold January morning, about six thirty a.m., I was in our church which was very dark. I was conscious of a person walking down the middle aisle to the altar, staying there for a few minutes in what appeared to be prayer. When the footsteps returned to pass the pew where I was in prayer, I called out an invitation to the person to join me.

"My name is Bill."

"My name is James."

"What's going on, James"?

"I am going to commit suicide."

"How are you going to do that"? I asked.

"I am going to starve myself to death."

He reached into his pocket and showed me fourteen cents. "That is all I have to my name." By now I am able to see him a little better. He was about thirty years old, dirty, long neglected hair, face hidden behind a long beard and he wore a torn, dirty winter jacket. Well, we both agreed that he would go home but come back to meet me at nine a.m. Prior to that time I was able to muster one of our core workers and one member of the St. Vincent de Paul conference. First order of business, after some coffee was a shower, shave and haircut. We were fortunate to have access to a shower facility in the White House, formerly the carriage house on what was an estate property. A trip to the Thrift Store produced a change to clean clothing. Now, the scene shifts to his home which was located in the heart of middle America on a typical street in almost any Long Island community. The modest, four room, one bath house was invisible from the street as it was buried behind years of overgrown foliage.

This once normal home of a father, mother and their one child, James, was now totally concealed in the heart of this middle America street. Now, the house was a candidate for a major overhaul, outside and inside. The roof had lost a number of shingles. There was a visible painting neglect of years together with broken windows and doors. An empty, rusty oil tank and an aged automobile of better days gone by rounded off the landscape. This was only the beginning. If Hollywood were to build a prop for a haunted house movie they couldn't have done any better. The living room with its soiled furniture was laced with a screen of cobwebs, covered like his face was, with grime. Now, we knew why. The electricity and water had been shut off many months before and James improvised with an old piece of metal as a stove to do his cooking. Lest I get caught up in the housekeeping, or lack of it, the most important component, the presence of relatives, friends, neighbors was missing. There were no living relatives except a lost contact aunt who lived in the city. There were no friends and the neighbors seemed to have left him in a type of solitary confinement. Maybe they were afraid of him. Well, Jesus, the wheels of charity began to turn as the baptismal calls to share their gifts surfaced in so many inspiring ways as they responded to the needs of James. Medical, mental health, barber, social security benefits, review negotiations with the utility companies; food, house cleanup and landscape repair work to let the sun in, all those blessings brought your love to a reality for James. Over the next six months there were frequent visits to a mental hospital where a short rehabilitation was necessary. Some cigarettes and a lunch at a nearby restaurant were most important to the rehabilitation process. We successfully negotiated a job opportunity only to have associate employees ridicule our young man to the point where he could not handle it. This was another missed opportunity for the community. Jesus, you are very aware of the number of retirement parties I am accused of manipulating. Well, at one authentic party James was there and added his comments to the guest book:

"Thank you for finding me in the Church."

Jesus asks, "Where is James now? Have you lost contact with him"? No, James has found himself in the Church doing volunteer work in the food pantry five days a week. On his fiftieth birthday fifty-two people from the community gathered to celebrate this wonderful human being that you have loved from his very beginning. Fifty-two individuals who were instruments in walking with him from the darkness of isolation to the light of community now love James very much. Thank you, Jesus, for the opportunity to be Servant Church.

"This was a beautiful ending. Do all of your experiences with charity and justice end up so well"? Jesus asks.

I am sorry to say, Jesus, not always. The big void is still social justice. I'll mention an experience that did not have such a happy ending. Julius was a graduate of a catholic university. He rose from the position of an executive trainee to senior management in an out of state corporation. Unfortunately, this young executive in his early thirties had a marriage of short duration. There were no children. Otherwise, it was a real success story. There were no health problems, no financial concerns, no drugs and no alcohol. But, something snaps for some unexplained reason. It is still a mystery to this day. He misappropriated twenty four thousand dollars from his employer in a way that was so open it was as though he wanted to be apprehended. Almost immediately he made a full restitution. The court trial decision results in no incarceration, no probation, no community service, no fines and yet there is one major problem. Julius could not find employment. Months of searching were fruitless. "Why"? Jesus asks. The pipeline is working against him. One mistake labels him for the rest of his life. I maintained compassionate communications with him as I tried unsuccessfully to open the heart of some CEO who would give Julius another chance. He finally took his own life with a revolver. The following note was given to me by a relative in the funeral home:

NA

> Mr. Mac,
> Thanks for being there for me. I wish I was more like you and had your faith and strength. It was great seeing you again and I appreciate your trying to help me. It meant a lot to me. The inner pain was just so great in the end and I didn't have the strength to make it back. Please pray for me and ask God to forgive me. I wish I had been smarter when I was younger and developed myself more like you. You're a great man.
>
> Thanks for your love and support.
> Julius

Jesus says, "Bill, that was a very fine tribute. He liked you very much, didn't he"? Jesus, I'm not sure that Julius knew that all of my faith, strength, love and support came from you. I am only your instrument. I am sure you have taken Julius to yourself.[14] But a problem remains. We are still living in a society that does not seem to provide a second chance, certainly not a third or fourth. You know, Jesus, in my seventeen years in your ministry I have come across only one employer who would give a first offender another chance in line with their talents and skills. Hopefully, this will serve as an invitation to some employers to understand that if they make commitments to love and forgive as you do, justice has to be an integral part of the sacramental life out in the world. In 1999 I understand this has been improved due to the booming economy. May it continue and be out of love after the boom. Jesus, I thank you for the opportunity to be a Servant Church.

Jesus encourages me, "How well I know Bill how you and all your mission associates have been and still are trying to build Christian, compassionate communities as my Mystical Body on earth. If you would please share some of your other experiences that might become an invitation to our brothers and sisters who for whatever reason have not heard my message."

....

14 John 14:3

Yes, I will go on. I hope these stories once and for all destroy the myth of there being no poor in our community. I also hope that they bring everyone to the reality that the boundaries of the poor extend well beyond economic stereotypes. In one way or another it is all of us who are poor and how we need each other. One time I had a request in the parish for a barber to shave a man in a wheelchair who was an amputee. A number of calls were unsuccessful. As I am in the habit of doing, I wrote a note to myself, "barber for Paul," and left it on the front seat of the car. While I was driving to teach a social justice workshop in a North Shore parish, I am chastising myself as to why I could not find someone to do it. On my way home from the class I again read my note, maybe it was a cue card. I thought what is the matter with you? Why can't you shave Paul? Well, I went to Paul's house instead of my own, and shared with Paul's wife the thought I had while driving. If Paul was game, I was, in attempting a first. Half way through the shave Paul looked at me and asked, "Do you know a priest who would come to see me"? Did I cut his throat? "I have been away from the Church for nineteen years." Paul received the sacraments and died a few months later in the company of his saintly wife who devotedly cared for all his needs over many years. Marcia was a wonderful example of a person with little time for the needs of the community, but who modeled you, Jesus, in the care of her husband as she helped him maintain his human dignity. Thank you, Jesus, for the opportunity to be a Servant Church.

Jesus expresses a concern. "This is so important. These are wonderful examples of what the Father and I want to see in our Church. Yet, so many of the men and women who were consecrated to our Love at Baptism seem to have drifted away. How do you think we can reach the Oneness that is our Will when there is so much division, so much splintering"?

Perhaps, Jesus, we are on to a missing link in the present structure. Certainly the stories represent the goodness that is the commitment of a number of people. Yet, I pray and hope that by telling these stories many more will be called to be vibrant participants in the charity of Your Servant Church. I also pray and hope for the days when they will connect the actions of charity to the causes of injustice and be an effective voice for change. We will have to look to the leadership—clergy and laity. What do we see? Is your lifestyle, Jesus, a model or just a nice narrative? Do the lost sheep see too much power, institution, bureaucracy, authority? Does modern day secularism, lifestyles, possessions, materialism, and consumerism blur the vision of solidarity with the poor? Forgive me, Jesus, for the long-winded response. Help me to your simplicity. Let me get back to more stories.

"I enjoy them very much. Please continue." Jesus replies as He sits back against the trunk of a shoreline tree.

This is another sad ending but an example of what can happen when individuals get caught up in forces counter culture to love or to support in the community. John was a thirty-five year old alcoholic who came to your Church for help. He was unemployed, homeless, and without any visibility of family or friends. He was struggling with a commitment to recovering, substantiated by a short period of dryness. He seemed to be heading in the right direction. We helped with the location of work and a room in a boarding house. One day I received a call from his landlady that she had not seen John for three days. She indicated that he was locked up in the room. I went with a volunteer to the house and persuaded John to unlock the door. As he climbed back onto the bed we had an opportunity to survey the emptiness of the room, the single bed, one chair and an unshaded light bulb hanging from the ceiling. On the floor at the side of the bed was a three quarter consumed bottle of raspberry brandy. Since John was not in any condition to discuss a recommitment to recovery we suggested some food and rest with the understanding we would revisit the following day. We left with the remains of the raspberry brandy as our companion. But the tomorrow never came. During the night John had gone to a deserted park area and hanged himself. Thank you, Jesus, for the opportunity to try to be a Servant Church. Would the ending have been any different if John had experienced a different Church in the earlier years?

Jesus appears to want to continue with the stories; "Bill, in those early years of your ministry did you ever have any experience with any brother or sister of mine who was suffering with AIDS"?

Yes, Jesus, I did. As a matter of fact there was a time in the early eighties when I received a call from the owner of an apartment complex. He had called to determine if the Church would help a tenant whom he was evicting for non-payment of rent with a footnote that the electricity had been shut off for the same reason. The Church assistance he sought was for relocation of the tenant. He also mentioned that the man was terminal with the AIDS disease. This last disclosure was the cause of a collapse of all of the support structure. AIDS was an unknown quantity carrying tremendous fear. It was a fear that was not only in the minds and hearts of the ever-dedicated core support team but also one that I too shared. I could not find one person to make the home visit until one of our registered nurses volunteered to go with me to the apartment. Louis was a forty-year-old black man living with Clare, a twenty-four old white girl. The apartment furnishings consisted of one dinette table, two chairs and a bed. That was it. Nancy, the nurse, took the young lady into the bedroom while I went to the kitchen with Louis to see if we could bring some kind of prioritized order to their needs, which were obviously many. Without spending a lot of time on the details of both assessments I should highlight a few of the most important. Louis was dying and medical attention was the priority. I was unable to locate an ambulance that was willing to bring Louis to a hospital. This was finally accomplished with the use of my own car. The hospital placed Louis in a room in a deserted wing. The fear and anxiety of the rest of the community was also there in the hospital. Louis died a few days after the last visit to him. Nancy brought the compassion and wisdom that was so important to the young girl. But I have to add another footnote, Jesus. When my conversation with Louis was coming to a conclusion in the kitchen, I stood up to shake his hand, but my hand was frozen. I couldn't raise it. Fear and anxiety were there again—in spades. Maybe it was the grace and example of your relationships with lepers (for the AIDS patients are the lepers of our day), that brought my hand to a firm clasp with his hand. Thank you, Jesus, for the opportunity to be a Servant Church.

I often reflect on the subjects of racial discrimination and prejudice. If a substantial number of our Church congregations had the opportunity to touch the pain of Louis and Clare, would not there be more conversions of hearts to charity and justice as a way of life, your way of life? Jesus, I think so. It has been a long morning. Why don't we have lunch. I brought a picnic basket with some sandwiches and fruit.

After lunch Jesus observes with a smile, "Bill, I think it is time to bring in some lighter, more humorous experience. Up to now this has been very heavy lifting."

That is a good suggestion, Jesus. We had an eighty-six year old widow who depended on different members of the Outreach support team to do her food shopping. When the shopping was completed you could depend on Rebecca to call the office with the same complaint. That person you sent today has cheated me out of four cents. Sometimes, it would be three cents or maybe six. A RENEW group of eight women provided Rebecca with one hot meal each day that they cooked in their own home. They filled a need until the town program exhausted the waiting list. In between that activity and three falls that required the police to break in and assist Rebecca, her deteriorating condition prompted the need for a home health aide. The Outreach support team included fifty-five women who were available to do "hands off" patient care. For the most part they were women who had serious income deficiencies and hence required a minimum hourly rate which was well below the going rate for custodial caregivers. Also, they were the only members of the Outreach team that received financial reimbursement. Well, Jesus, let me get back to Rebecca. Early on in the employment of home aides I was informed that the efforts that were being made to have Rebecca pay the caregivers were of no avail. She absolutely refused, assuming that this was the responsibility of the Church. Well Jesus, I was asked to go and see what I could do. My ten minutes at the foot of her bed was a strikeout. No way was she to pay them. I am sure she used the same rationale on the home care as she did on the shopping. Finally, I looked her directly in the eye and said, Rebecca, look at me. See me? It's Bill. If you don't pay these women I am going out that door with them and that's it. We will not be back. You are on your own. After a few minutes of silence she sheepishly invited me to open a dresser drawer and there to my shock was a drawer full of old Social Security envelopes with a total of twenty-eight hundred dollars in cash plus nine Social Security checks which were not cashed. Thank you, Jesus, for this opportunity to be a Servant Church. Even when we are so busy, if only we could find an hour a week to visit the Rebecca's we would find ourselves at the foot of the cross in love with Jesus.

Jesus wants to broaden the scope of who are the poor with this question, "As you have reflected on my lifetime I am sure you must recall the criticism I received for my compassion towards prostitutes. In your Outreach experience did any prostitutes ever come to my Church for help"?

Yes, Jesus. There were a few times when they did. I remember one young lady in her thirties who in the earlier years had graduated from the parish school. Although she was from a family of affluence and support, she got caught up in the drug and alcohol world of the Vietnam era. Eventually she ended up on the streets of New York with a homeless shelter for her address. The beautiful ending was a telephone cry for help to the Outreach office. I visited the young lady with another volunteer. The shelter was so crowded with bed against bed. I like to feel that our compassionate interest in her demonstrated by a one hour visit after the two hours on the LIE brought her to the decision to leave that life behind. A demonstration of a recommitment to a normal life back in the community of her early life and the eventual reconciliation with the family brought your Light into what was darkness. If I am committed to your way of life, Jesus, there can be no exclusions, not even a prostitute. Thank you, Jesus, for the opportunity to be a Servant Church.

"Bill, all of those stories you have told relate to love and compassion on your part and also that of your community. You and they share their gifts, gifts of my Father, with so much hurt, pain and brokenness which exists in not only your parish community but in all communities of Long Island. Thank you for sharing them in hopes that they will be an inspiration to any parish community that is not aware of the scope of the needs and the sacramental responsibility to respond. Beautiful changes have taken place in the life of the individuals, both the served and the servers. But what about systemic change"? Jesus asks.

Jesus, You are right on to one of the main objectives of this testimony. As I have said, we are a very generous, charitable people. Yet, there is still ample room for more and more people to make the commitment to share the gifts of their baptism in charity with others. The great void is justice, in changing systems that effect large numbers of people.

"Is there any progress being made on justice issues at all"? Jesus asks. "For example, when I was on earth I welcomed everyone regardless of race, creed or color. It was the inspiration of my Spirit that led our bishops to witness my Truth on the subject of discrimination. Again Bill, I ask you, is there any progress"?

Very little, I am afraid. Let me give you some examples. About fifteen years ago our Outreach was asked to respond to the food needs of some Salvadorians who were living in our community, (if you could call it living). They had fled political persecution in their homeland. There were twenty-four in all including two families with six month old infants. They were in a two-bedroom home with one bath. The sleeping quarters were the floors with blankets for the most part, which extended to the concrete floor of the cellar. NIMBY, Not in my Back Yard, was evident all around them in spite of their exemplary behavior under inhuman conditions. The absentee property owner collected twenty-two hundred dollars a month in rent. These circumstances were duplicated in a number of towns around the Island. Later on, probably about five years later, there were so many cries for help from individuals and families who had fled political and/or economic persecution that Catholic Charities trained a staff under the identification of New

Neighbors. Their mission was to go out into the communities and respond with Parish Outreach volunteers to the economic and legal needs of these new neighbors who came from Central and South America as well as Europe. It is now the eve of the new millennium, almost sixteen years later, and very little has changed in attitudes while the needs of our new neighbors have multiplied one hundred fold. We recently witnessed an effort to run twenty-five to thirty men out of town with the unwelcome words, "go back to Mexico where you came from." The doors of the house in which they were living were closed to them by many of the people in the community. The local parish church was the only welcome sign in the colds and snow of December, a timely remembrance of the Bethlehem scene two thousand years ago. Sorry, Jesus, but this is the way it is. On another occasion I visited some property out on the East End of the Island with some volunteers. Our first greeting was two cesspools overflowing over the landscape. Fortunately or unfortunately this badly in need of repair house was well hidden from the main highway although it was visible to a three hundred and fifty thousand dollar home resting on a knoll about one half a mile away. The bathing facility was limited to an improvised shower on the side of the house. There must have been some pretty cold showers in the winter but I congratulate the twenty-four Mexican young men who lived there on the property for their cleanliness. Eighteen lived in the house and six in a well-ventilated barn as it slowly fell to the ground. This tragic scene was a secure seventy-five miles from the professional ownership and its lucrative return on an investment. Not only distance but also a property manager kept the owner away from the opportunity to touch the pain of these young men from Mexico. The only connection was the financial traffic of one hundred and fifty dollars a week, from each man, if they were working. So you see, Jesus, although a few are managing to be the Servant Church as they try to respond to the material needs of the many, the major problems of a welcome climate, a change in the hearts of our society and the legal implications of our immigration laws remain as a major challenge. What a difference could have been made in the lives of these men if the owner saw justice in its fullest as an important part of his Judeo Christian responsibility.

"Bill, what about my Church? Where is the leadership, Jesus asks, on these issues that effect so many of my hurting brothers and sisters"?

For starters, one way of working towards some solutions is in small prayer groups that are inclusive, the servers and the served. There were three groups that were formed in our parish community several years ago.

"Excellent, that brings people together with me." Jesus seems to express his support.

One consisted of a group of men and women who met for thirteen weeks around the Spiritual Exercises of St. Ignatius. There was representation from different ethnic and religious backgrounds including a woman who managed to escape death in the Holocaust. Father Pete and I facilitated the exercises which give a person an opportunity to bring faith to work in their family and in the market place."

Another group I will identify as the HUD prayer group. HUD because they all lived alone, except one, in a government subsidized housing project. The group, all women, consisted of a fifty-one year old black Baptist on a Social Security Disability Grant, a sixty-eight year old black Baptist dependent solely on her Social Security check, a Presbyterian widow and mother of eleven grown children, a thirty-one year old Catholic mother of an infant who was killed in an accident, a fifty-five year old Italian American parishioner with a heart condition and a forty-nine year old Italian American inactive Catholic. When you were on earth, Jesus, you were always so compassionate and supportive to women. Maybe that is why only women, with the exception of John, were at the foot of the Cross. The group met weekly on Wednesdays and with some member of the Outreach support team. For one hour they would reflect on some passage of Scripture, relate it to the signs of the times, recite the Our Father followed by prayer intentions for the community and close with some refreshments.

"Bill, doesn't this destroy the myth that all they want is something that is free"?

Yes, it does, Jesus. A similar group with the same inclusiveness met in another section of the community. There was a spirit of solidarity in the individual crosses each one carried. I have to come to the commitment that those crosses are my crosses. It is interesting, Jesus, that so many different backgrounds melded into so much common and sacred ground. I hope that relating experiences like this will destroy once and for all the other myth, we don't have any poor in our community.

Jesus continues his interest. "Again I ask, where is the leadership on the issues of social justice"?

When You say leadership, Jesus, for a moment we should separate the clergy from the laity but only to illustrate where it is at currently. Then, we must step back into solidarity. I would like to use the issue of the homeless as an example. There was a great experience of church leadership where with the support of the pastor, volunteers and funds from the thrift store, a two-bedroom apartment was rented as a transitional shelter for men. The purpose was to take the men off the street in a crisis, identify their prioritized needs, and help them to respond and walk with them to a point of self-sufficiency. Here is the content of one such group that lived together in the shelter. Each one had come at different times to the Outreach:

- Jim, a seventy year old alcoholic
- Harry, a fifty-one year old alcoholic, terminally ill with throat cancer and evicted by his wife
- Louis, a twenty-one year, old mentally slow, disowned by his parents for some bizarre behavior
- Tom and Ben, eighteen year old black twins who, prior to admission to the shelter, had lived for thirty days in an abandoned car after their parents deserted them

Beyond the material and health needs, each of them regardless of age, had a hidden hunger for some spiritual nourishment. This was witnessed by their voluntary participation most evenings in the Liturgy of the Hours at five p.m. The life of the saint of the day was often of interest to them. Then, there was the time that Catholic Charities opened an apartment in the basement floor of the seminary for a Hispanic homeless family. The practical needs of the father, mother and two small children were met with the support of three neighboring parish outreaches. I would have to admit to you, Jesus, that this effort was not without controversy within the leadership. Neither the parish community shelter nor the seminary effort was meant to resolve all of the homeless and related problems. However, Jesus they were intended to witness your teachings and to be a sign of a Servant Church in communities throughout Long Island. They were not to be seen as something unique and unusual. Sometimes there are some efforts that seem to continue and survive only with your grace. The presence of clerical and lay support is not always so visible. There are times when an effort is made to be that sign of the Servant Church only to receive opposition from leadership circles.

"Give Me an example," as Jesus asks for more specifics.

One such effort was a parish community that opened the doors of an auditorium in freezing weather several years ago only to receive some criticism. You know, Jesus, when I traveled around the diocese a few years ago I would find a number of your churches locked up in the daytime. Yet another church in the same geographic area remains open. How much has changed since then I don't know. Another example is "Casa dela Paz," a home for homeless refugees which is under the supervision of Father Bill[15] who at the time lived there with the people. In this small house in a well-populated area of Wyandanch at any one time you are apt to find up to twenty individuals who erroneously fit a stereotype for police suspicion and vigilance. Amongst the residents on my visit there was a single Mexican female parent with her young children, one boy and two girls of early school ages. Also in residence was a forty-four year old man from El Salvador with a seri-

....

15 Reverend William F. Brisotti, Administrator, Our Lady of the Miraculous Medal Parish, Wyandanch, New York

ous throat illness that left him unable to work. My conversation with Father Bill was most inspiring.

"Working with the poor is a sacrament."

"If we don't touch the pain of the poor, if we don't make real concentrated efforts to teach priests, future priests, the laity, and especially the youth about the mission with the poor we are denying them the sacramentality of the Cross."

"If we succumb to the counter culture climate of the people who are not ready for this we should take the Cross down."

"It is easy to be Catholic in name but very difficult to be one of the followers of Jesus."

"Great things are done a little at a time."

This is another realistic model but I have to say that the love and the care of the persecuted from other lands is not an option if I say in prayer on Sunday that I am a follower of you, Jesus. You know, Jesus, I wondered while I was there how much support Father Bill receives by the presence of brother priests, bishops, laity or is he there alone with you and the residents? I would have to admit that while I was there it was an experience of the sacred, of the Cross, of a Servant Church with an unwelcome population. A few years ago I was in the Holy Land of your life here on earth. I knew I would never be the same again after walking in your footprints. Father Bill and I agreed that when you walk in the footprints of the poor you never will be the same again.

Jesus reminds me, "Whatever you do for one of these least brothers and sisters of mine, you do for me."[16] As the sun sets over the trees surrounding the lake, we call it a day. Jesus affirms the work and the dedication of the Parish Social Ministry volunteers and the members of the St. Vincent de Paul Conference. He concludes with this question,

"Can an ordained priest live in the 21st century just as I lived"?

1 John 2:5-6

....

16 Matthew 25:40

CHAPTER 5

CHALLENGE

Jesus went around to all the towns and villages, teaching in their synagogues, proclaiming the gospel of the kingdom and curing disease and illness. At the sight of the crowds, his heart was moved with pity for them because they were troubled and abandoned like sheep without a shepherd. Then, he said to his disciples, "The harvest is abundant but the laborers are few, so ask the master of the harvest to send out laborers for his harvest."

Matthew 9:35-38

People from a number of the towns and villages of Western Suffolk have gathered to hear Jesus in his opening reflection around the scripture reading: "If anyone wishes to come after me he must deny himself and take up his cross daily."[17]

Then, Jesus expresses a concern to me. "You have spent a substantial amount of time up to now on the great works of charity throughout your parish communities. It is my desire to bless each individual who in one way or another has shared their gifts with our poor. Each one is helping to build the Kingdom on earth. But you know, Bill, there is so much more to be done. Hopefully, by telling the stories that you have related to me, many more of my brothers and sisters will be led to new opportunities to serve in the Servant Church. Bill, do you think you now should go beyond the

....

17 Luke 14:27

charity and address the justice issues and their causes? There are still so many troubled and abandoned sheep without a shepherd."

Yes, Jesus, the experiences of this testimony have to be connected with justice. Often, our presence to a hurting person results in freeing them from the chains of a crisis, and the movement to the grace of a state of self-sufficiency. Unfortunately, we have too many situations where we need more than the one on one guidance and support. These are the situations where systemic change is necessary, where more than one voice must be heard and where we need the solidarity of the voices of the troubled and abandoned, together with the voices of those who serve them. We need to hear more from the pastoral voices of the leadership, both ordained and lay people. This was the challenge of yesterdays and is still the challenge of today and the tomorrows to anyone who professes to be your follower. Hopefully, the year acceptable to the Lord will be two-thousand, the new millennium, a 21st century jubilee year.

Jesus interrupts, "These are noble thoughts but is there not a need for a substantial amount of ground work to be done as you try to motivate my brothers and sisters from where they are now on the Cross carrying mission of justice to where my Father intends it to be in the Kingdom building"?

Jesus, I have to pass an opportunity for brevity, which is not one of my long suits, and go back to the yesterdays. I have to carefully avoid even the smallest taste of cynicism or criticism and only in a constructive climate learn from the past. It was in nineteen-ninety that I recognized that to move the social justice agenda we needed trained leadership, ordained and laity, to bring your justice teachings, the teachings of the Second Vatican Council to the many who are not hearing it. This is the reason that in January of this year I left the training of small interested groups in parishes under the sponsorship of Catholic Charities to reach a larger audience with my testimony as the vehicle. We needed help with the "how to" in those earlier years of the nineties. We need the same help today.

"What did you do in nineteen-ninety"? Jesus asks.

I made a decision to go out to the pastors with two subjects on the agenda. To address the first subject, I wanted to make them aware of the different and multiple services that were available to their parishes from Catholic Charities if they had the need and desired that kind of support. The many stories which I shared earlier were potentially their stories. This information was well received. The support was identified as assistance to the parish in building truly Christian compassionate communities as the Body of Christ.

- building: slowly, a brick upon a brick.
- truly: the TRUTH of the Gospel.
- Christian: Jesus, the model of a proper balance between prayer and action.
- compassionate: walking at the side of the hurting person.
- communities: the resources of the community, the served and the servers, together as the Body of Christ.

"What was the second subject"? Jesus asks with obvious interest.

I started with this declaration of purpose. I have come to pick your brain. Yes, we do very well in the overall efforts of charity as individuals, as a church, as a secular community or as a nation. The problem rests in the movement of the justice agenda where unless there is a well-defined self-interest item we are making little progress. What are we not doing that we should be doing? What are we doing that we should not be doing? What new ways are there that are different and that we should explore together? Supporting the key question around the justice issue were some related observations and concerns of mine.

One was a prior effort we had made to build a relationship with government where we had a conference on the subject of the causes of injustice and how to effect change. There were twenty-four invited participants including a state senator, staff members of an assemblyman, two pastors, parish outreach coordinators, parish outreach advisory board members, two Protestant ministers, Catholic Charities parish outreach developers, the executive director of the

Society of St. Vincent de Paul with two conference presidents, one Hispanic, single female parent with four small children and a recovering alcoholic business man. Both of the latter had experienced support from their parish communities to bring about change in their lives. The immigration and alcohol issues that both of them experienced had a direct connection with government funding. Our presentation included:

- our Judeo Christian social justice roots in relation to the poor of our times.
- the teachings and lifestyle of Jesus.
- one hundred years of Catholic Social Doctrine and teachings.
- the social justice documents of the Second Vatican Council.
- John Paul II's messages related to justice.

"How did the government people respond to this agenda"? Jesus asks.

Jesus, the response of the senator as spokesperson was honest, direct, and challenging.

"You are good people doing great work and I praise you. But, you come to Albany either seeking support for existing legislation or recommending new laws related to your social justice agenda, but you do not represent the large majority of Catholics nor of Christians.

Your message is not being heard by the majority of Catholics or by other individuals of different religious persuasions. Politics is a game of numbers. You really do not represent my constituency. So, my recommendation to you is to go back to your communities to educate and train the people on Catholic Social Justice Teaching."

Jesus comments: "That was very direct. Were there any other subjects during your visit with the pastors"?

Yes, Jesus. Another subject centered on the priesthood and two related thoughts that came out of the Second Vatican Council. One was: "The Shepherd and Bishop of our souls set up his Church in such a way that the people whom he chose and acquired by his blood should always, and until the end of the world, have its own priests for fear Christians would ever be like sheep that had no shepherd."

The other was; "It is the duty of Christian people to cooperate in various ways, both by the earnest prayer and by other means available to them, to ensure that the Church will always have those priests who are needed for the fulfillment of her Divine Mission."

Twenty five years later we were experiencing a decline in the numbers of priests and vocations.

"Has that changed"? Jesus inquires.

I am sorry to say, Jesus, the decline continues.

"How many pastors did you meet at that time"? Jesus asks.

I met seventy-three over a period of a year and a few months. There were an additional seventeen who were initially contacted by letter with the agenda and then with follow up telephone calls which remained unanswered. This is not noted as a criticism but rather as a nudge to encourage us to review the modern day burdens of management and finance that are being carried on the shoulders of our pastors.

"Did you reach any conclusions about the priesthood"? Jesus continues his interest.

Well Jesus, it seemed to flow around struggle:

- struggling priests.
- the numbers that were leaving the priesthood.
- a climate where some pastors were of the opinion that the decline could be of a Divine design.
- struggling laity.
- as they search for new meanings of the inner life.
- desire for new forms of prayer.
- is there something else?
- are we different?
- do we look like Jesus? prayerful? action that supports and assists our hurting brothers and sisters in crisis?
- confrontation with the authorities to address the causes of injustice.
- the struggle to implement change.

Then Jesus, there was this question: "Is the Roman Catholic Church on Long Island seen as the Church of the poor"?

"That question must have stirred some controversy." Jesus observes.

Healthy controversy, yes. We agreed that this is a very complex concern but at the same time questioned ourselves as to whether or not as Church—all the people—we may have lost the Social Justice dimension of our mission.

Could it be that too many have lost or never had a sensitivity and commitment to the need for a properly balanced spiritual dimension—contemplation—with the service and action for change components?

As the People of God have we lost the will to address the causes of injustice and bring about the changes necessary to reflect the God mandated respect for the human dignity of every person?[18]

- Should it receive increased energy overall?
- Is Social Justice seen as a ministry?
- Is Social Justice seen as an essential element of evangelization?[19]

"Bill, do you think this point of relating social justice to being a good Christian was understood then? What about at the present time"?

Jesus, No and No. A little later we will experience the position of our bishops in 1992 with me on the subject.

To wrap this up Jesus, in answer to your last question, I think that these important factors should be subjects for further exploration with a priority urgency now, as I felt they should have been at that time. They are as follows:

....

18 Genesis 1:31

19 John Paul VI, Evangelization in the Modern World, 1975

- many of the pastors were most appreciative of the purpose of the visit, namely as an opportunity to obtain their opinion rather than a directive as to the way to do things.
- the average time of each visit was an hour and fifteen minutes including two visits where a pre-announced fifteen minute time restriction was converted to an hour of interested dialogue.
- there was general acceptance to the validity of the presentation.
- the overwhelming majority stated that they never had very much social justice education and training. This included undergraduate, graduate or on any form of continuing education.

You know, Jesus, it was interesting then, and it is at the present time, how many ex-priests and ex-seminarians come to Catholic Charities or other social agencies to explore opportunities to become directly involved in the Social Justice Mission of the Church.

"Bill, did you get an answer to your earlier question? Is the Roman Catholic Church on Long Island seen as the Church of the poor"?

Yes Jesus. They did not see any significant identity of solidarity with the poor but they all would like to have that relationship to have become a reality.

"What other common denominators were there in the visits"? Jesus asks.

May I summarize some of my personal observations as a result of these meetings?

"Please do." An interested Jesus replies.

These pastors are the same men who fifteen to fifty years ago said yes to your call to leave everything behind and follow you.

They want to be the shepherds of the flock, the spiritual directors of your people.

They recognize and accept the relationship of the Gospel values to the social justice mission of the Church and they see prayer as an integral and intensive part of it.

"What else"? Jesus patiently asks.

Social Justice education and commitment in its fullest has

to begin with them, the pastor and parish staff, before going out to the people. It is the opinion of your Jesuit social justice leader, Father Walter Burghardt, that "If your Church is serious about the Social Justice agenda, the continuing education of the clergy, deacons, religious and laity is absolutely necessary and that without it there will be little or no movement." Father Walter and his team from the Woodstock Theological Center at Georgetown University have been traveling all over the United States facilitating five day retreats to priests and deacons that connect the prayer and spirituality with the social justice teachings and suggest the opportunities for action in both service and advocacy. During the past eleven years I have presented workshops to hundreds of parish people in their respective communities. This curriculum takes one from the importance of prayer, then connecting the Judeo/Christian justice teachings to touching the pain of someone.

"What has been the reaction of those parishioners"? Jesus asks.

Jesus, the reaction of these participants without exception is, "We never heard this before—why"? They are energized for more study and involvement in their communities. There were other thoughts that the pastors shared with us that should not be overlooked.

"What were they, Bill"?

Jesus, they were of the opinion that a substantial part of the laity need the knowledge of the basics of their faith before they can be directed towards social justice. It would seem that the Pastoral Formation Institute was and is one answer to the training of leadership for the basics.

There should be a strengthening of the social justice leadership and implementation at the level of the bishops, the clergy and laity. At the pastoral level it is almost a numbness on the one hand, but an openness and a searching for some creative direction on the other.

Not many parishes are recognized with a vibrant and balanced relationship between:

LITURGY & SACRAMENTS * RELIGIOUS EDUCATION * SOCIAL JUSTICE

There was a lack of constructive social justice dialogue at all levels within the official church as well as within the community, namely other churches, government, education, the professionals and the marginalized. We were not reaching out.

Jesus says, "Please go on."

Jesus, it is amazing that I covered so much in an hour and fifteen minutes with the pastors.

Continuing the dialogue with the pastors—we were not reaching out to our youth and involving them in the social justice mission through their prayer/spirituality connected with the teachings and then the opportunity to touch the pain of the poor in charity and justice.

"Bill, is there any progress with the youth"? Jesus asks.

Very little. Our mission is so counter to what they experience. There is a minimum of social justice communications in its totality in the Catholic media as it relates to gospel values. Examples are the Long Island Catholic, television, Internet and/or Church publications, all of which could be valuable exposures for our youth. We need it there before we reach out to secular communications who seem to have a beat for the negative but rarely the many positive activities around charity and hopefully some day around justice.

"Are there any climates that you feel are unhealthy and need attention"? Jesus asks as he guides the conversation.

Yes, I feel we have to change the anti-institution, the "downtown" identity, the anti-Catholic Charities and/or St. Vincent de Paul perceptions. We have to remove the pressures of day to day administrative and financial duties of pastors. I do not sense any change since that time when I met with the pastors. They were not trained for these responsibilities. We have a substantial amount of lay talent available to find solutions. We have to reduce the demands of the heavy volume of "downtown" mail. More programs, no matter how well intended, are not always the answer to conversions and evangelizations. Too often, all of this melded together results in frustration, confusion and even anger.

This runs the risk of placing the pastor in the very category of the oppressed that we are committed to free. This is the basic foundation stone of social justice.

"Are there any other experiences you wish to share from the parishes or diocese or beyond"? Jesus asks.

I will answer your question about other experiences. What was happening beyond the parish and diocese on the national scene? Critical is the ever widening gap between the rich and the poor and it is not confined to the local community. It is a state, national, and, yes, global tragedy. The so often misunderstood and at times unwelcome Catholic Charities is one of the voices of the poor. It is very interesting. Shortly after the closing of the Second Vatican Council the leadership of National Catholic Charities, now Catholic Charities USA, embarked on a study to discern the direction of the Council and chart the course ahead for Charities, both nationally and locally. This study became known as the Cadre study. The main focus centered on community, which is a major theme of the Second Vatican Council. Catholic Charities was started in New Orleans by a dedicated group of nuns in a parish community one hundred and fifty years prior to the study. Over the span of those years Catholic Charities became more and more a central bureaucratic agency. The Council and the Cadre study were saying—go back to the community. One of the firsts, if not the first, diocese to respond to this direction was Rockville Centre. How fortunate for me to have had such close guidance from two of the pioneer leaders in the implementation of this renewed ministry in the parish community. I must express my deepest gratitude to Father Pete and Father John.[20] In those early days it was known as Parish Outreach in the three pilot parishes. Today, it is recognized as Parish Social Ministry in some ninety parishes.

"Bill, you say Parish Social Ministry. Does this mean that all ninety parishes are actively involved in the ministries of charity and justice"?

....

20 Ibid. 2, 3 page iii

No. That would not be true. The gap between the direct service of assistance to needy brothers and sisters, both spiritual and material, and an active advocacy involvement for systemic change is very wide. I must recognize that to have experienced the present level of direct service development it would not have happened without the involvement of a large number of individuals being given the opportunity to be an active part of a Servant Church with the support of the pastors. I say a large number collectively but it is a small number related to the potential. Jesus, this is the audience I prayerfully hope to reach with my testimony. It is a journey that has a long way to go.

Jesus then asks me but he makes eye contact with each person from Western Suffolk. "There is so much mention of the poor within Church circles, in prayer, and in activities of service. Who are the poor in your times"?

The poor are the counterparts of your time on earth. I have to turn back to you for the answer. "Go out quickly into the streets and alleys of the town and bring in here the poor and the crippled, the blind and the lame." The servant reported, "Sir, your orders have been carried out and still there is room." The master then ordered the servant, "Go out to the highways and hedgerows and make people come in that my home may be filled."[21] Maybe a community that proudly states that it has no poor in its community, bases this observation on a narrow geographic area. They have to go beyond the front door. Remember the early story about James? They have to look not only around their own street but also the streets where the economically poor live which may be the alleys of this point in time. They have to look at their own family. Maybe, even in their own home there is a hurt or pain or brokenness. The crippled and the lame can be those with a physical impairment with no access to medical care. Maybe, they are figuratively crippled and lame by burdens placed on their shoulders by a blind society.

....

21 Luke 14:15-24

Jesus, there is also another activity where we could respond to your invitation to fill your home, namely our liturgies, be it Sunday or a diocesan hierarchical ceremony. Help us to change the congregation from a primarily one ethnicity, one level of social and economic status, to a mix of people. This would include every income level, welfare recipients, ex-offenders, prostitutes, the downsized unemployed, the depressed, the hard of hearing, the runaways, the pregnant teenager, the people of different religious persuasions, the faithful choir of twenty to twenty-five percent believers and the seventy-five to eighty percent who have left us for whatever reason. All brought together as ONE, as you prayed that we would be ONE with you and the Father and the Spirit. All melded together in a common prayer of gratitude to be participants in the Servant Church, served and serving, all melded together in a common prayer of praise and glory to you, Jesus, to the Father and the Spirit.

Jesus is ready to conclude with this question.

"Can a town assembly woman live in the 21st century just as I lived"?

1 John 2:5-6

CHAPTER 6

THE CROSS

> *Come to Me, all you who labor and are burdened and I will give you rest. Take my yoke upon you and learn from Me for I am gentle and humble in heart. For my yoke is easy and my burden is light.*
>
> *Matthew 11:28-30*

"Bill, that was a nice day yesterday with the people from Western Suffolk. Is my invitation to come a support to you in the commitment to the mission"?

Jesus, I have tried to make your sufferings over the plight of the poor, my sufferings. I have reflected on the signs of the times and the challenges I faced during the pre-Vatican and post-Vatican council years of this century from personal experience, from experience with the Church and from experience of the world. Many of these experiences have been very positive, often inspiring. Others reflect more of a struggle. Still others relate to deep hurt and pain. Sometimes the burden was self inflicted, sometimes imposed from without. You invite the burdened, and whatever our role we are all burdened, the served, the server, to take up as a yoke on our shoulders, a yoke of listening to your teachings and a yoke of obedience to those teachings. It is there that I will find rest. It would be understandable if I chose to stop here. If I chose to congratulate myself on the great burdens that have been lifted from the shoulders of some poor people, a kind of dual satisfaction of rest for the served and the server. But, Jesus, how well you know I cannot and

I must not stop. I must stay on the journey as you did to the Cross. The invitation to continue the journey goes out to everyone who up to now has been a part of it and to the large majority of our brothers and sisters who have disconnected but are still hungering for the relationship with You. They may be individuals who are experiencing some form of brokenness or others who are experiencing a call to serve as you served, Jesus. The invitation goes out to all, the inner circle and the outer circle[22] to begin this premillennium journey at the foot of the Cross. If I am to recognize the scope of the hurt, pain and brokenness that surrounds me, as I have tried Jesus to provide this focus, and I am to commit to being part of the vision of a new Servant Church in the next millennium, my serious discernment tells me, I repeat, I must first go to the foot of the Cross. However, not as a nice object of a narrative about an event of two thousand years ago but a TRUTH with all the gory and horrendous human details melded together with the divine in the doctrinal facts of faith. I have to share your sufferings, Jesus, physically, emotionally, lovingly, before I return to the communities to address the causes of the burdened, and strive for ways to bring them rest as an important sacramental part of being one of your followers.

Jesus offers a suggestion, "Bill, it might be helpful to go back for a moment to reflect again on the subject of who I Am. At the Last Supper you will recall I prayed to the Father for a return to the glory with Him that I had before the world began."

You mean, Jesus, that you existed before planet earth was created, before celestial bodies were positioned and before the creation of Adam and Eve?

Jesus replies, "That is the Truth. At that time I also prayed to the Father. As the apostles believed in who I was, they didn't choose to belong to the world any more than I belonged to the world.

....

22 Twenty to twenty-five percent active and seventy-five to eighty percent who have disconnected for whatever reason.

Yet, it was our will that they had to stay in the world. They had to continue with the work that I had begun."

Well you know, Jesus, that many of our brothers and sisters find it most difficult to be the voice for change, to stand up against the secular world that is so counter culture to your teachings, a secular world that at times doesn't seem to have any interest or desire to be consecrated in the TRUTH.

"Bill, do you remember that at that same time I made two promises to them and to you"?

What were they, Jesus?

Jesus replies to the question; "That in the world you all will have trouble but take courage because I have conquered the world and that you had to have faith in my prayers to the Father to protect them from the evil one. At the same time I prayed for you and your contemporaries who will believe in me in the years after, because of my teachings and your witnessing my life."

What I am hearing you say, Jesus, is that I should follow you in faith that you did exist in the Oneness of Love with the Father before the world was created. I should in faith believe that you, at the command of the Father, assumed our humanity and conquered the troubled world when you willingly accepted the suffering and death on the Cross. In this divine act of Love carried out in your humanity you atoned for my sins, for all the sins of humankind from Adam and Eve to the last person who will be on this earth at the end of time. Mind boggling! Who but God Himself could accomplish such a covenant?

"So you see, Bill, this is where you have to begin if you are to bring about the necessary conversion of hearts. It is not minds but hearts that have to be converted. You have to believe that regardless of how rough the justice road will be, and you will probably be wounded, I am there with you as I was with my apostles. I pray for you now as I prayed for you that night in Jerusalem two thousand years ago." Jesus challenges me as we walk in a wooded area of the North Shore.

Forgive me Jesus if I sound a bit commercial but it is not a new thought with me. I think we have done a poor job of marketing the Cross with all of your horrendous, mental and physical sufferings as well as who you are and what you did for me, for us, for everyone. If only every person would go to the foot of the Cross at the dawn of each day to reflect on who you are and the cause of your suffering and death, what a different world it would be. The marketing plan has to move Good Friday from one day a year to three hundred and sixty four days a year, (three hundred and sixty-five in leap years) leaving twenty-four hours for a glorious celebration of your Resurrection.

"Bill, who do you say that I am"? Jesus asks me once more.

You are Jesus, the Son of God.

"Maybe if together we reflect a bit on three points it will be helpful to begin to experience some real movement on the road to justice." Jesus suggests.

Please, Jesus, go on. What would the three be?

Jesus compassionately replies; "First, on the Cross to whom are my arms outstretched"?

I know the answer to that question would be everyone, all of those who came before us, all of those who will come after us and the six billion strong of the now.

"True. It might be helpful though to identify those individuals whom you would like to reach with the invitation to walk with us on the road to justice, as they witness the gospel by word and action." Jesus asks for more clarity.

I feel, Jesus, that as I wish to be a part of the rebuilding of a Servant Church there are a number of wonderful people out there that have not heard the message. They don't understand that you are there on the Cross—as John XXIII said—"You have been hanging there for two thousand years." Your arms are outstretched in an invitation to them to take up the counter culture yoke that will help them move from a posture of ignorance, indifference or even fear in speaking out on the sensitive issues of injustice.

Your arms are outstretched to those individuals who feel that interfering with the creative hands of the Father in the womb is a personal matter only, without any moral or legislative responsibility to publicly witness the TRUTH.

Your arms are outstretched to those individuals who claim to respect the dignity of the human person. Yet, anyone who has taken the life of another is an exception and the death penalty is the only just decision.

Your arms are outstretched to those individuals who claim to respect the dignity of the human person. Yet, anyone who has outlived a societal established quality of life, such as, the elderly, the terminally ill, the mentally disturbed is an exception.

Your arms are outstretched to those individuals who agree that all human persons are entitled to the inalienable right to vote, free speech, food, shelter and work. Yet, they do not accept those individuals who come to the land of the Father (not our land) from their home in a foreign land as they flee political and/or economic oppression. Jesus, remember, this is commonly recognized as NIMBY (not in my backyard).

"Yes, Bill, I know I have heard it before." Jesus replies.

Your arms are outstretched to those individuals who live in error as they oppose the bishops for connecting the social justice with the building of the kingdom of God. It is too secular and belongs outside of God's plan.

Your arms are outstretched to those individuals who live in error as they stereotype the poor in terms of color, race or ethnic background.

Your arms are outstretched to those individuals who oppose the Church taking an active role in applying Gospel principles of justice to contemporary situations with appropriate political action.

Jesus adds; "You know Bill, that my arms are also outstretched to all those individuals who wish to be my disciples in the next millennium.

My arms are outstretched to touch the pain of the infant boy or girl in the womb who are crying out for the same opportunity to live as those involved in the decision of their death enjoy."

Are there others, Jesus?

"So many more—yes—so many more." Jesus replies.

Tell me who are they so that I may touch their pain with you? I ask Jesus.

Jesus goes on.

> *"My arms are outstretched to the twenty-two year old black man who sits in a solitary cell on death row awaiting the fatal needle of a lethal injection.*
>
> *My arms are outstretched to the eighty-one year old grandmother with Alzheimer's who is no longer useful.*
>
> *My arms are outstretched to the fifty-one year old businessman in intense pain with terminal cancer.*
>
> *My arms are outstretched to the institutionalized thirty year old man who has been disturbed mentally since birth.*
>
> *My arms are outstretched to the twenty-two year old Hispanic twins who are isolated from me by the curtains of individualism, riches, and possessions, that are drawn around them by the cultures of today's society.*
>
> *My arms are outstretched to the Haitian family of five children and their parents who are the economic victims of a society that endorses the separation of the religious and social dimensions of life and will not accept the teachings of the church.*
>
> *My arms are outstretched to the twelve year old black girl in the big city who is denied adequate educational standards in a decent classroom environment.*
>
> *My arms are outstretched to the thousands of men, women and children in the inner city who suffer oppression and powerlessness while the more affluent members of society speedily drive past or quickly flick the TV remote button to blot out the misery.*
>
> *My arms are outstretched to the twenty to twenty-five percent of the faithful and the seventy-five to eighty percent who have left us who may be part of an apathetic community that victimizes itself by its failure to be a voice for change in the voting booth.*

> *My arms are outstretched to the families who live on the riverfront polluted by the conscienceless industry that created the conditions.*
>
> *My arms are outstretched to the twenty-four individuals in Kosovo who were martyred and buried in a common grave because they sought peace."*

Jesus, I am overwhelmed by the scope of injustice that exists all around the world, around our nation and in our community. Earlier I reflected on so much individual hurt but in the spirit of charity and with your help we were able to free individuals from the chains that bound them. But what you have identified is too much. What can I do?

Jesus replies, "Have Faith. Whatever you ask the Father in my name will be given to you. For everyone who asks, receives, and the one who seeks, finds and to the one who knocks, the door will be opened.[23] Where is your faith? Do you remember now? Come to the foot of the Cross and share the sufferings of the oppressed, share the sufferings of the oppressors. Ask in their name for relief from these sufferings because you have sought the causes of their injustice and found them. You have knocked on the door of freedom and I have opened it. If you are serious about the mission of justice this is where you must begin. See yourself. See the world."

What I seem to be hearing is that before I engage the society of our times in the dialogue and debate over the issues that are contrary to your teachings that there are certain steps I should take to get started.

Jesus answers, "Yes, Bill. Too often, well-intentioned people, both laity and clergy, give communications with me a fast brush. They hurriedly move right into the work or at the least, reflect momentarily on a prayer recitation. Bill, this is heavy lifting from a human standpoint. It is a call from me from a divine standpoint.

....

23 Luke 11:9-10

If one chooses only the fast brush they will do some good. You might call it secular humanism. However, if they choose quality time in prayer, they will do great works. Remember another promise from the last meal I had with my apostles. 'Whoever believes in me will do the works that I do and will do even greater ones than these because I am going to the Father. Whatever you ask in my name I will do also, so that the Father may be glorified in the Son. If you ask anything of Me in my name I will do it."[24]

Jesus, when You were on earth You were a teacher. I need you now to be my teacher. I need your guidance and direction to enter the twenty-first century. If I am truly Christ-like, I should be very serious about experiencing some substantial movement in social justice. There has been very little up to now. I affirm the relatively small group of individuals who have tirelessly worked at it. But I need your help in how to reach the large majority who are not hearing the challenge for a massive conversion of hearts that will be the solid rock of the foundation of a truly Servant Church. It is a Servant Church in which the lost sheep find what they seek and satisfy their hidden spiritual hunger.

Jesus replies as He looks out at the world; "It is so good to find this faith on earth before I return. Remember my concern two thousand years ago when I publicly wondered if there would be any faith on earth when I returned.[25] It is nice to hear your call to increase your faith as the apostles asked me then. I say to you as I said to them, if you have faith the size of a mustard seed, you would say to this mulberry tree, be uprooted and planted in the sea and it would obey you."[26] "Bill, from your own experience, what would you suggest for those individuals who have felt a grace filled energy to go on"?

....

24 John 14:12-14
25 Luke 18:8
26 Luke 17:5-6

Jesus, I would suggest three parts for consideration in their commitment:

One: a commitment to listening prayer
Two: a commitment to detachment from anything that stands in the way of one and three
Three: a commitment to attachment to my teachings and to touch the pain of those who cry out to be freed from the chains that bind them.

Jesus suggests; "Perhaps it would be helpful to them Bill, if you would expand a bit on these important steps that brought you to where you are in the justice journey."

May we hold that until a later time. For now, I would prefer to reflect on our talk this morning.

"Till then, Bill, give some thought to this question, Can an automobile mechanic live in the 21st century just as I lived"?

1 John 2:5-6

CHAPTER 7

LISTENING

Then his mother and his brothers came to him but were unable to join him because of the crowd. He was told your mother and your brothers are standing outside and they wish to see you. He said to them in reply, My mother and my brothers and sisters are those who hear the Word of God and act on it.

Luke 8:19-21

As we leave the eleven o'clock liturgy Jesus refers to the scripture passage as perfect for the priest's homily.

Jesus, you asked me to share some of my own personal experiences on prayer. That is good timing for to do so makes a good introduction to the subject of "Listening Prayer."

Jesus says, "I hesitated to make the request as I didn't want to embarrass you. As you know, prayer, I should say listening prayer, is so important. Angela, your wife, tells me that often you don't listen."

She is quite accurate although my attention span and concentration is getting better, I think!

"Go on." Jesus replies, as he avoids any further awkward discussion.

Well, it would be helpful to divide this subject on "Listening" into three parts:

- My own personal experience that you requested.
- The cries of the poor.
- The voice of the Church.

Somewhere in the early lines of this testimony, I made reference to that time on an early morning walk when you prodded me to give as much thought to my spiritual life as I was giving to my post-Marine Corps physical condition. Then, there was a long period of twenty-eight years when you were silent, or maybe you were speaking to me but like Angela told you, I wasn't listening. I like to think that you intentionally left me alone to carry out my family and work responsibilities by your word and your example. Perhaps, the silence of your voice is a clue to a style of prayer. You will remember earlier when there was a reference to how this Pre-Vatican Council Catholic prayed. It was a style which was very mechanical, concerned with quantity, very private, and, to say the least, very busy. In truth, there was no time to listen because of too much self absorption, too much self preoccupation in prayer, too much self fixation in prayer, in short, too much self and too little you, Jesus.

"What changed all that"? Jesus asks.

That is an important question. What changed all that! I would have to say that although I was involved in many acts of charity, the prayer life was more packaged, more canned, if I may use that sort of expression. To make a more sacred reference to the reason, I would say it was not well grounded. It began to be more grounded when my spiritual director recognized the emptiness of my prayer life to date and encouraged me to start slowly, very slowly, with Matthew, Mark, Luke and John. This took close to two years of listening to a small piece at a time and trying to relate what you were saying to the signs of the times in which I was living. Then, I found myself being pulled back to Luke and starting all over again.

"Why do you think that happened"? Jesus asks.

Now Jesus, you know the answer to that question. Was it not because Luke wrote so much about your love, your mercy.

"Where did this second time around with Luke take you"?

When I started Luke this second time, I was prompted to write about my reflections, again small sections at a time.

Jesus interrupts. "But had you not taken an early retirement, one of many more to follow that people kid you about, at the time when you were re-reading Luke"?

Yes, Jesus. I had actually retired a year and seven months early and volunteered to begin a Parish Outreach at my home parish of St. Mary's in East Islip. It was during those early months that I had received the spiritual direction to begin the Four Gospels. When I went back to Luke and started the writings, I don't remember it being identified as journaling, in contemporary jargon. But, I guess it was and I didn't know it. At about the same time, influenced by my thirty-seven years in the retail business, I was searching for a logo that would identify the Parish Outreach. Early on the writings were flowing into a pattern of:

TRUTH— the actual scripture message
LOVE— as relating to the signs of the times we were living in
CHANGE— our Spirit led action to result in change

Our parish school art instructor developed the logo, which to this day is used in all notices and publications. Thank you Jean.[27]

Jesus then asks as he sips on his second cup of Starbucks. "What ever happened to your journals? Sorry Bill, your writings"?

Well, you know Jesus, I was encouraged by two priests who read parts of it to send it to a publisher for possible publication. In the end I had sent it to five. The feedback was complementary but their concern was that I really was not known. One publisher said that if I were dead, my writings would have life. In the meantime, Jesus, thanks to your grace I am still here. I have distributed the book to all fourteen adult members of the family and nine grandchildren when they reached Confirmation age. At the moment there are twelve to go. Am I drifting off the subject of your question?

....

27 Jean Donnelly, former Art Teacher at St. Mary's Grammar School, East Islip, New York

"Not really. Continue. Where did this lead you"?

It brought me, led by the Spirit, to a conclusion that if we are serious in the Church about witnessing the Gospel as the foundation for the Social Justice mission we must start at the foot of the Cross in prayer. We must grow in "Listening Prayer." I heard very little from you, Jesus, except the curbstone incident, until I entered into a discipline of quality time in prayer, reading small bits, relating them to the world around us and then listening for your direction. Then and only then things began to happen. Most important I became closer and closer to you. My hearing through my heart improved immeasurably. The give of yourself that I referred to early on was really the beginning of a true charity and justice journey in response to your call to follow you. It moved me from a cul de sac to a long wide-open road. Over the seventeen years that have followed, I have heard you seven times in my heart and always in the presence of the Blessed Sacrament.

- At moments of confusion, I am with you always. I will tell you what to do.
- At moments of temptation with negative concerns for the poor, serve with love.
- At moments of basking in glory and praise that belonged to you, Jesus, be a silent lover.
- At moments of inquiring as to where the justice road was going, you spoke not in words but through the image of the twenty-one black crosses.
- At moments of serious concern for the life of our Church, pray incessantly.

Remember I didn't know the meaning of the word incessantly and I had to go to a dictionary. I should have known from St. Paul.

- During early morning moments while shaving, love perfectly, wait patiently.
- At moments of your peaceful presence, live in the present moment of your Presence.

"Before you go on, is there anything else you wish to add to your own prayer experience"? Jesus asks, as he guides the conversation.

Yes, Jesus. In the past few years I have become more and more conscious of the injustices that are plaguing us, in our communities, in the nation, and throughout the world. At the same time there is the paradox of the hunger for a spiritual dimension in so many. The following prayer was a result of a feeble effort on my part to help people in their justice concerns. The Good Friday Crucifixion Meditations at St. Mary's, East Islip, that you have led me to share with others for the past fifteen years were the catalyst for my development of this prayer.

Come and share my sufferings, now as then. At the dawn of each day see my arms outstretched on the cross embedded in the top of the global world.

See my Body covered with the red blemishes from the Agony in Gethsemani where

I anticipated the physical pain and suffering connected with the Father's call to atone for the sins of all humankind.

See the scope of evil in the world from Adam and Eve to the end of earthly time, violence in so many different forms.

War, murder, suicide, destruction of the work of the Creator in the womb, physical and mental abuse of the elderly, of spouses, of children, political torture.

Adoration of the false gods of the flesh, consumerism, materialism, destruction of minds and bodies with drugs and alcohol.

Breakup of families, corruption in government, in business.

The plight of the poor in the shadow of the rich.

The oppression of widows, children, orphans, aliens, refugees.

The defection of some of my priests.

The negative effect of some behavioral patterns by members of my Church on my other brothers and sisters.

See all of this evil in the wounds of my flesh caused by each stroke of the scourging.

See all of this in my bleeding head wounds from the thorny crown.

See all of this in my bleeding wrists and my feet, from the nails driven deep into the wood of the Cross that holds me outstretched in love to every person.

See how all of this intensive pain and suffering is only exceeded by the pain and suffering of rejection—to my love-to the love of the Father-to the love of the Spirit.

Each dawn after you have experienced the fire of my Divine Love move on to your daily tasks and make a special effort to address the causes of injustice in prayer and in practice.

So, Jesus, you have carried me a long way from the pre-Vatican Council Catholic who was so content with the very private love affair with you, and sometimes some tears, to a deep understanding of the scope of the Trinitarian love for me and to bring that love to myself first and then out to others. You broke down the wall of privacy. You encouraged me to go public, to bring the light out from under the table.

Jesus goes on. "Bill, your recognition that anyone wishing to go down the long road of justice should begin with the inner self and the relationship with me is so important. I am the model. As you know, I prayed incessantly, now that you know the meaning of the word, to the Father, as I wanted to maintain the relationship that I had with him before the world began. It is important that your brothers and sisters reflect on that truth, as it will give a lot more impact to their reflections on my passion and death, on my Resurrection, on the why of it all. In prayer also I hear an invitation within the voices of the poor as they cry out to me and to you to come to them, to give them strength, to heal them. Bill, what is being heard today from the poor, the marginalized, the oppressed"?

I am afraid Jesus, that little has changed. I hear the voices of individuals asking for food and there are the dedicated who respond in charity to them. I hear the voices of the neglected homeless who need shelter, the lonely single parents who are mostly women, the isolated AIDS patients and the unknown mentally ill. There is a small, dedicated group who respond with material, financial assistance and presence to them. But little has changed in the hearing of other voices that should be heard in our listening prayer. They are the voices of the victims of:

- Racial discrimination, at times in our own congregations, communities, and/or corporations, in prisons where physical brutality is often a reality, by red-lining in mortgage banking, job opportunities, access to adequate medical care and overall stereotypes that make a person of a certain color or ethnic background or gender, an automatic suspect as a target for prejudice.
- Denial to life from the muffled cries of the infant within the walls of the womb to the depressed cry of the terminally ill seeking assistance with suicide as an only alternative in their minds, to the other targeted population who have been identified by society as no longer useful.
- Denials to their inalienable rights, locally, nationally, globally to vote, to free speech, to a choice of where they want to live free from economic and/or political oppression.
- Worry and fear for loss of financial and economic security in their old age in the most prosperous country in the world.
- Substandard education whether it be in the quality of teaching or in overcrowded classrooms, or deteriorating buildings.
- The poverty of those who have fallen through the cracks with the ever widening gap between the rich and the poor.
- Oppression, the children dying from poor nutrition and hunger.
- Oppression, the children victimized in our own communities as well as nationally and globally by desertion of a parent or parents.
- Economic oppression in third world countries that are being strangled financially as they go deeper and deeper in debt.

Oh Jesus, there is so much to be done in distributive justice. This is my prayerful concern for the new millennium. Help us to look to the inner circle of the faithful first, before we go out to the outer circle and beyond to change hearts. We are, and rightfully so, deserving of criticism on the subject of human rights when we establish the subject as a condition of trade with a foreign country, while we tolerate and encourage forms of discrimination in our own country or city [Except China where we ignore human rights because McDonald's and Disney toys are more important].

"My teachings are so perfectly clear on all of those subjects. Why are not people with the power, which is everyone, responding to them"? Jesus asks.

Your brothers and sisters are not hearing it. So, there seems to be no motivation to act on it.

"What is it that you want them to hear in listening prayer"? Jesus asks as he looks out the window on the community of Huntington.

Well Jesus, I have tried to help them from my own personal experience in listening to what you wish to say to them directly. I have just encouraged them to listen to the voices of the poor in their prayer. I should now ask them to listen to the voice of your Church in prayer, listening prayer.

"That is very pleasing to me. Go on." Jesus encourages me.

It would probably be helpful if I shared a teaching pattern on justice that I have used in the past with small groups. This is what I repeatedly hear people complain that they are not hearing. It begins with your two greatest commandments: to love the Lord God with all your heart, with all your soul, and with all your mind. This is the greatest and the first commandment. The second is like it: you shall love your neighbor as yourself.[28] My neighbor includes every single person whose voice was heard crying out above.

Then, Jesus, I take them to Genesis. God created man in his image; in the divine image he created them, male and female he created them. God looked at everything he had made and he found

....

28 Matthew 22:34-40

it very good.[29] The male and the female can be the victims of oppression whose voices we hear everyday crying out for help.

Jesus endorses with these comments, "What a wonderful place to begin to build a foundation for social justice education. Perhaps you should mention the related passage from the book of Leviticus in the Old Testament. At this point in time it might also be helpful to remind our brothers and sisters that all of the words of both the Old and New Testaments are the inspired work of sacred authors."

Yes, Jesus, that would be appropriate. Remember how I mentioned earlier that in the pre-Vatican Council years we were not permitted to read scripture for fear of misinterpretation nor discuss the subject of the Trinity. What a tragedy! Now, back to your suggestion related to the Book of Leviticus. In a world with so much hunger every ear should hear your message spoken through the author.

> *When you reap the harvest of your land, you shall not be so thorough that you reap the field to its very edge, nor shall you glean the stray ears of grain. Likewise, you shall not pick your vineyard bare, nor gather up the grapes that have fallen. These things you shall leave for the poor and the alien. I, the Lord am your God.*[30]

This is God using Moses as an instrument to tell the Israelite community then—to speak to our communities, our nation, the world now—that charity and justice are required components of holiness as a disciple of Jesus.

Be holy, for I, the Lord your God, am holy.[31]

Jesus asks, "Bill, you mentioned earlier the plight of the aliens

....

29 Genesis 1:27-31

30 Leviticus 19:9-10

31 Leviticus 19:2

and refugees who are not welcome in your country. Was this not a problem in the time of Moses"?

Yes, Jesus, it was a problem and as you know Moses addressed it.

> *For the Lord, your God, is the God of gods, the Lord of lords, the great God, mighty and awesome, who has no favorites, accepts no bribes, who executes justice for the orphan and widows and befriends the alien, feeding and clothing him. So, you too must befriend the alien for you were once aliens yourselves in the land of Egypt.* [32]

Jesus reminds me, "In the closing year of the twentieth century have you forgotten that you had parents and grandparents that too were aliens as they passed through the gates of Ellis Island"?

Jesus, that reminds me of the cliché, "They are one generation away from a pick and shovel but they have forgotten it."

Jesus chuckles. "Sometimes a little humor can be more effective than a serious tone. How true! It is of concern that what I am hearing you say is that people are not hearing about the roots and the richness of the social justice teachings."

It takes a bit more exposure than perhaps one Sunday once every three years. It is my hope that before I conclude I will have an opportunity to express some specific thoughts with your help for our brothers and sisters to consider. As you know, Jesus, there are a number of references in song in the Book of Psalms that are direct hits on justice for the poor. If I had a good voice I would sing the verses but let us be content to continue to listen in prayer to the voice of our Church:

> *Yahweh is close to the brokenhearted; and those who are crushed in spirit he saves.*
>
> *For the Lord hears the poor, his own who are in bonds, he spurns not.*

....

32 Deuteronomy 10:17-19

> *For he shall rescue the poor man when he cries out, and the afflicted when he has no one to help him.*
>
> *He shall have pity for the lowly and the poor, the lives of the poor he shall save.*[33]

Jesus, as you know, there is so much more on the subject of justice in the Old Testament. Maybe, I could reflect on three more from the prophets, Jeremiah, Isaiah and Amos.

One: Only if you thoroughly reform your ways and your deeds; if each of you deals justly with his neighbor; if you no longer oppress the resident alien, children, orphans, and the widow, will I remain with you in this place in the land which I gave your father long ago and forever.[34]

Two: Take your wrongdoing out of my sight.
Cease to do evil.
Search for justice.
Help the oppressed.
Be just to the orphan.
Plead for the widow.[35]

Three: I hate and despise your feasts,
I take no pleasure in your solemn festivals,
When you offer me holocausts, I reject your oblations and refuse to look at your sacrifices of fattened cattle,Let me have no more of the din of your chanting, no more of the strumming on harps, But let justice flow like water and integrity like an unfailing stream.[36]

We must remind ourselves twenty-six hundred and fifty years later as to who are some of the most oppressed people of our time.

....

33 Psalms 34, 69, 72

34 Jeremiah 7:5-7

35 Isaiah 1:16-17

36 Amos 5:21-24

They are the individuals and families from other lands seeking the freedom they were denied in their homeland:

- Children dying, from Harlem to Africa, from lack of food.
- Families with no access to medical care.
- Orphans of slain parents in Angola.
- Widows in our country who struggle for survival with an inadequate Social Security benefit to pay for the basic necessities of life, while our Congress debates endlessly without resolution.

Jesus, we are at the moment, listening in prayer to your voice, the voice of the poor, and the voice of your church. The challenge to our clergy, religious and laity is to address the response to these teachings. How do we become a voice for change? This is a sacred open moment in the life of the Church. We must not fail.

"You won't, Bill. At this point why don't you go on to some of my teachings while I was on earth, my teachings around justice. What can your brothers and sisters listen to in prayer that might be helpful to them if they choose to make a commitment to live just as I lived"?

There was the time that James and John were looking for a place of prominence in eternity when you shot them down to the delight of the other ten apostles. Yet, you brought them together in a circle around you for some pastoral guidance and told them, "You know that those who are recognized as rulers over the Gentiles lord it over them and their great ones make their authority over them felt. But, it shall not be so among you. Rather, whoever wishes to be great among you will be your servant. Whoever wishes to be first among you will be slave of all. For the Son of Man did not come to be served but to serve and to give his life as a ransom for many."[37]

Jesus adds, "Bill, you know I tried throughout my public life to be a model that would help people. No one promised that it

....

37 Mark 10:42-45

would be easy. That is why I encouraged you to begin at the Cross. From there you will be able to carry the crosses with the aliens, the refugees, the children, the widows. You will be able to use authority represented in the collective voices of the served and the servers in harmony with my voice for change. Is this not the way to use power"?

Thank you, Jesus. It is so helpful to me and I am sure to others. When I listen in prayer to your words you seem to give me the grace to relate the teachings to the signs of the times in which we live.

Many times, Jesus, we struggle with our choices of how much we give of ourselves to your church. How much influence do we have on the role of government in our lives, be it private or in community, all from a standpoint of finance, materials and time? Do you have any thoughts?

Jesus replies, "Maybe this will be helpful to you as you listen in prayer. One day I sat down in the synagogue where I could observe how the members of the congregation were contributing to the temple treasury. There were many generous people, as you have told me that there are today, who gave large sums of money. At the same time there was a poor widow who gave two small coins worth two cents. I called my disciples to me and told them, 'Amen I say to you, this poor widow put in more than all the other contributors to the treasury. For they have all contributed from their surplus wealth, but she from her poverty has contributed all she had, her whole livelihood.'[38]

Then there was the time the scribes and chief priests were doing their undercover work in their desire to build the evidence that would lead to my execution, to get rid of me as I was threatening their authority. In a false climate of affirmation, dripping with craftiness, they tried to trick me with a loaded question, 'Is it lawful for us to pay tribute to Caesar or not'? I asked them to show me a denarius and responded to their question with another. Whose image and name is on the coin? Caesar's, they replied. Then, repay

....

38 Mark 12:41-44

to Caesar what belongs to Caesar and to God what belongs to God. There were no more questions, only silence."[39]

Jesus, it seems as though both of these incidents should be helpful to me in the struggle. Both seem to have a connection with my responsibilities to actions of charity and actions of justice. It is of little consequence when I make financial donations to a worthy cause from what is left over after I buy stocks and bonds, or at the supermarket when I buy two or three cans of food for the poor after filling two carts for my own appetite, or the donation of six shirts that I don't need any more since I have a wardrobe of eighteen. Yet, in charity I feel pretty good about myself. As for justice what I hear is twofold.

One, my obligation under law is to pay my income and property taxes, no short cuts, whatever the rules dictate.

Two, there is a role in justice that belongs to the Caesars. When problems exist that are hurting the dignity of people and they cannot be resolved in community then we should turn to Caesar, our elected representatives, local, state or national, and be a voice for change. This is what we call the principle of subsidiary where the dialogue participants go up the responsibility ladder until a level of resolution is reached. If Caesar at a local, state or national level is needed, so be it.

Jesus observes; "I know Bill that you are planning to conclude your testimony on the voices of the Church. Maybe, before you do, you could address this problem of Church and State that I hear so much about. What should be heard in prayer on this subject."

As you know, Jesus, the Second Vatican Council discussed this subject at great length as they redefined the relationship of the Church to the State.

There should be no human act that is not governed by moral standards and the Church has a designated responsibility to teach in all matters related to those standards. Yet what we hear over and over is that religion has no place in politics. Liberals and Conservatives

....

39 Luke 20:20-26

alike espouse it. There was an incident in one of our parishes while a priest was teaching a principle of social justice in his homily. A parishioner stood up and cried out, "That's political and you have no right to bring that to this liturgy." With six other "Amens," the seven men and women stood up and left the church. This is one incident. Yet, precisely, it is the problem. We are not hearing the message with the regularity it deserves. There seems to be little or no energy for a public theology that brings the doctrine into the reality of everyday. Our national and diocesan Catholic Charities have the energy but their active participation is relatively small in comparison with the overall potential of a well trained constituency as disciples of Jesus.

Jesus tries to help with these words. "You know, Bill, that the people of ancient, early American and contemporary history have addressed this subject. Do you think it would be helpful to spend a little time on it"?

Well, Jesus, I am not sure how great my history knowledge is but I will give it a shot. Let's start with Aristotle who asked:

What is a human being?

What is the good life from a standpoint of others?

How do you organize a community to make a good life possible for all?

He linked politics with praxis in doing things for the community.

Plato concluded that good is good because it is good and evil is evil because it is evil.

The fathers of our nation based their revolutionary case against the tyranny of King George on the Word of God:

> *We hold these truths to be self evident, that all men and women are created equally, that they are endowed by their Creator with certain inalienable rights.*

Jesus, this is a religious statement.

"What about some examples that are a little more contemporary"? Jesus asks as the Huntington fire sirens interrupt the quiet of the room.

That is a good suggestion. Take Benjamin Franklin. He gave financial support to all religions because they contributed toward goals of good ethical standards.

The Abolitionists based their efforts to abolish slavery on the Word of God.

In Lincoln's Second Inaugural Address, he spoke to both the Union and the Confederacy, "both of you read the same bible and pray to the same God and evoke his aid against the other."

Collective bargaining supporters based their arguments on the Word of God. So do the advocates for racial equality.

In 1968 the crew of Apollo 8 read from Genesis as they orbited the moon.

Is there any other word that the unborn can cry out for help to live than the Word of God?

Jesus encourages with, "Bill, don't be discouraged. Listen to the teachings of our Church who has every right to interpret the true meaning of scripture, Old and New Testament, as it relates to the signs of the times in which you are living. Proclaim my Good News as I repeatedly encourage you to do. My story is not limited to Christians. Share it with our Jewish brethren, with Hindus, with Buddhists, with Muslims. I love them all. I died for them all."

Well you know, Jesus, when we think about it, one didn't have to be Russian to read Tolstoy and one didn't have to be a Hindu to read the life of Ghandi.

Why don't I bring this listening to the voice of the Church to a closure. Maybe I have raised sufficient interest in our conversation up to now so that our brothers and sisters will not only read, but in prayer, discern what the social justice teachings are saying to them at this point in time. They are directed at so many contemporary problems that can all be solved. They cover issues related to labor, reconstruction of the social order, social progress, peace, development of peoples and evangelization. It goes from Pope Leo XIII one hundred-eight years ago to John Paul II and from bishops' conferences to papal councils. They are so rich, so full, so related to the building of the kingdom here on earth. But first, I have to recognize that the efforts to strive for justice are not an option for me. They have to be alive and vibrant in me because I am a disciple of Jesus. He died for me. I love him very much.

As we leave the Huntington Conference Center, Jesus watches in amazement as a twelve year old girl uses the mouse of the computer. On the screen he reads: my brothers and sisters are those who hear the word of God and act on it. Then Jesus asks. "Can a supermarket clerk live in the 21st century just as I lived"?

1 John 2:5-6

CHAPTER 8

DETACHMENT

Filled with the Holy Spirit, Jesus returned from the Jordan and was led by the Spirit into the desert for forty days, to be tempted by the devil. He ate nothing during those days and when they were over he was hungry. The devil said to him, If you are the Son of God command this stone to become bread.

Jesus answered him, It is written, one does not live by bread alone.

Then, he took him up and showed him all the kingdoms of the world in a single instant. The devil said to him, I shall give to you all this power and their glory; for it has been handed over to me and I may give it to whomever I wish. All this will be yours if you worship me.

Jesus said to him in reply, It is written: You shall worship the Lord, your God and him alone shall you serve.

Then, he led him to Jerusalem, made him stand on the parapet of the temple and said to him, If you are the son of God, throw yourself down from here, for it is written: He will command his angels concerning you, to guard you and with their hands they will support you, lest you dash your foot against a stone.

Jesus said to him in reply, It also says, You shall not put the Lord your God, to the test.

Luke 4:1-12

As Jesus walks with me through a vineyard in Mattituck, I asked him about the incidents. It must have been some experience. Was that the end of the devil? Did he bother you anytime after that incident?

"Most people will remember the above quote from scripture but may not be conscious of the closing line that "he departed from me for a time."[40]

"Bill, what does that suggest to you"? Jesus asks.

That would suggest that the devil came back again at you. You know, Jesus, that the devil is not the subject of everyday conversation. A Cardinal[41] in Rome recently acknowledged that many modern day Catholics may no longer believe in the devil. He stated that this was a serious fault in religious education. When there is a brutal murder like the recent one where a black man was chained to the rear of a truck, maybe there will be more sensitivity to the reality of an evil one. The chained man was dragged for a long distance with an open sewer pipe finally severing his head. Now, the horror of this incident brought many individuals to the conclusion that the perpetrators had to be possessed by the devil. What about ethnic cleansing in Kosovo! What happened in Columbine High School in Littleton, Colorado! Is there room to conclude otherwise?

"Bill, do you think the Cardinal is right"? Jesus puts me to the test.

I think, Jesus, that the existence of the devil is part of our Catholic faith and doctrine.

Jesus keeps the subject going. "Would it be wise to recognize and reflect on many of the saints and church leaders who lived lives very conscious of the existence of the evil one. For example, have you had any experience with the life of my brother, Ignatius of Loyola"?

It is interesting that you mention Ignatius. There is probably

....

40 Luke 4:13

41 Cardinal Medina Estevez, Vatican, Rome, Italy

no saint in the history of your Church that has had more influence on me personally than Ignatius. Would you want me to go into some of the details? I am forever conscious of not boring you with meaningless or unproductive verbiage.

"Bill, don't apologize. By all means, tell us the story."

Well, Jesus, in 1959 I accidentally read in a magazine, that there was a book written by a Jesuit priest.[42] It was called *The Spiritual Exercises of St. Ignatius.* I bought the book and over a period of several weeks I had a great and moving experience that has stayed with me to the present day. Ignatius developed a series of scripture meditations and exercises where Ignatius leaves no doubts about the existence and battle between the powerful forces of good and evil. Maybe it would be helpful to pick up on this struggle from three places: personal, church and world. What are the things from which I should be detached—the church? the world?

"That would be helpful, I am sure, to your brothers and sisters, but before you do, you had come across some thoughts around Pope John XXIII's experience on this subject."

Yes, Jesus, he is another good example. There is no doubt that he shared the conviction on the doctrine of the evil one and there is no doubt that he took steps to prepare himself for the combat. Early on, he chose a spiritual director and confessor.[43] He searched for a man who was not only holy but also learned and prudent. He made his confession every Friday at 3:00 P.M. He took the time out of his very busy schedule for it. He saw it as a way of reviewing his life, week by week, in the darkness of the evil one and the light of the Holy Spirit.

"Are you aware of any specific struggles that John experienced"? Jesus inquires.

Yes, Jesus. There is one that I would like to mention. It was prior to the Council. Pope John was very conscious of the opposi-

....

42 Reverend Louis J. Puhl, S.J.

43 Monsignor Alfredo R. Cavagna

tion that would come from some of the cardinals during the preparatory period to the implementation of the Council. He wanted the dialogue to be more pastoral than dogmatic. How well you know, Jesus, how much of the energy for the latter was evident. John recognized this anticipated struggle with these words. "Oh, I know what my personal part in preparation for the Council will be," and, after a pause, "I will be suffering." John XXIII is a great example for everyone in the Church who is involved in the social justice mission. I will suffer when I run head on into opposition from clergy, the religious, or the laity. They will either be forces that are hidden or up front. Regardless, I will suffer. Jesus, our counter culture movement will not be without suffering. How well you know, Jesus!

"Bill, you mentioned there were three areas you would like to address relative to the existence of the evil one."

Yes, Jesus. It would start with my own personal experience. The Ignatian exercises probably are responsible for my beginning to recognize the reality of the existence of some kind of diabolical energy. The exercises planted the seeds of the reality of an ongoing, never ending struggle between good and evil. It was an evil force that was sometimes very subtle and sometimes bold. Most important, it was a long way from a narrative in a textbook. To this day the scriptural reflection related to the signs in our own time, and the examination of self have been a most prayerful experience. It leaves no doubt in my mind that there is a devil and he is forever on the prowl. A few years ago, I gave him a name—Breakers.

"Bill, why did you ever do that"? A curious Jesus asks.

Jesus, the reason was that he was, is, and will be forever, trying to break in and influence me in some covert manner that will take me away from you.

"Bill, are you suggesting that you have to do battle with him"?

Yes, a lesson learned from Ignatius, perhaps it came from his military training. The devil tries to work you over so there was no reason for Ignatius or the men and women of this age or the future to expect immunity from this diabolical experience.

Then Jesus asks. "What has been your experience with recognizing his presence? Do you hear his voice? Does he E-mail you with his temptations? Does he work through others"?

Jesus, these are all good questions. It would probably be helpful to take a moment and look back at what brought me to this point in my testimony. Led by the Spirit in the beginning, I took a general appraisal of the signs of the times. This was followed by a review of the challenges that were experienced: personal, the church and the world, in both the pre and post Vatican Council eras. I concluded that after reflecting on a multitude of experiences with the hurt, pain and brokenness that exists in our communities there was a need to involve more people to reach out and touch the pain of so many more.

Jesus replies. "My grace will be with them always. I cannot guarantee that they will not be wounded. When they try to live their lives as I lived, they will suffer, especially when they stand up to the authorities to advocate for change. Perhaps the wounds will be inflicted by friends and maybe even by relatives. So often very good people who want to become involved with the ministry to poor people rush quickly into the doing. When they do, it is an invitation to burnout.

"Everyone must always be reminded that this is the work of the Father. Just as he sent me down to earth to be the Instrument of Love, He now calls on them to walk in my footsteps. Without me they can do nothing."[44]

"Go on, Bill."

The next building brick that I see, after prayer, is the need for detachment. The first questions I have to ask myself are: What gets in the way? What do I have to get rid of? What is the excess baggage? Once on that road I have to become very adept at recognizing the

....

44 John 15:4-5

voice of Breakers that may be personal or maybe through a third party. As to the first question, What gets in the way? Here Ignatius' three kinds of humility were helpful to me. Early on, it is that commitment that if I had all the promises made to me that were made to you by the devil, I would hope to never consent, in fear of disturbing my relationship with you. As to the second kind of humility, I am to avoid any inordinate attachments to riches over poverty, honor over dishonor, long life over a short life. The only objective was to discern what was God's will and do it, anything else, get rid of it. Third, if and when I attained one and two then I would pray for the grace to imitate you. I would prefer to be a servant to your poor than being rich. I would endure insults for that posture rather than honors. I would not mind being treated by the world as you were treated.

"Bill, doesn't this sound a bit idealistic and heroic in this contemporary world? Is it not more suited for religious or cloistered men and women"?

Forty-five years ago, Jesus, I would have said "yes." But, as you know, these exercises, modified, have become a way of life for me. Modified in that I have found that the commitment to the three kinds of humility can be made and witnessed without interfering with family responsibilities. You work just as hard to provide food, housing, clothing, education and medical care for your loved ones. The modification is that materialism at a level over and above what is needed is the excess baggage. It is what I have to get rid of. It should never become the priority. In some dark days you were always there to provide the support, the light, and the grace. Jesus, I hope I haven't wandered off the track. Maybe, it clarifies a bit the meaning of this necessary component of detachment. Of course, your grace in the post Vatican years led me out of the "save your soul" era into a deeper level of faith that you saved my soul by your death on the Cross. There is another modification of the exercises of Ignatius that was made by a Jesuit by the name of Father Lonergan. It can be very helpful to anyone who is willing to make the commitment to the social justice mission, as a true disciple of Jesus.

- Be free in a life of prayer.
- Be attentive to the data of injustices.
- Use intelligence to understand the data.
- Exercise reason in making judgments.
- Accept the responsibility to do the right thing.

As to how I think the devil works, I will give you some personal experiences, then some others with the Church and then the world.

Jesus says, "Please go ahead if you think it will be helpful to your brothers and sisters. Why don't you and I sit down for a few minutes and enjoy a few grapes."

That is a good idea, Jesus. Now, listen to the cunning Breakers and his subtle invitations to pull me away from following you. Many, many times the attack comes after an involvement or considered involvement with the poor. Several years ago when I was at my parish doing the outreach work, there was a twenty-five year old white male by the name of Patty who, as an infant, probably had whiskey instead of breast milk for he was forever intoxicated. He traveled with his second cousin from the same genes. In the years that I knew him we helped him with food, shelter and an occasional effort at recovery in a detox center, but these experiences were always short lived. One night Patty arrived at the Outreach office about 6:00 P.M. After he rang the bell and I recognized his "happy" face through the door window, I invited him in. It took only a few moments to assess his condition. I called the Catholic Charities Talbot House to inquire about a possible vacant bed, which thankfully, was available. Now, this was probably Patty's third or fourth trip to detox. So, you can see, Jesus, he was trying. I then called the local taxi to come and take him to Talbot House. It was the commuters' rush hour so they requested that I bring him to their office two miles away and between train arrivals they would take him to Talbot. About one mile into the trip Patty started pounding on the dashboard with both hands in accelerated rapidity. Without any warning, other than some strange groans, he turned on me, grabbed my throat and started to shake me. It was probably a drunken expression of affection, although at the time my thoughts were anything but. Jesus, it was your strength that enabled me to bring the car to a halt and free myself from his grip at the cost of a few buttons on my coat. I left the car, called the police from a local business phone, (I don't believe in cellulars), and after a total explanation of the situation the police took Patty to his detox appointment. After the police left, it was the subtle Breakers, you are wasting your time, at great personal risk, with the likes of Patty. They never change. Keep your distance.

Jesus asks, "Did you ever see Patty again"?

Yes, Jesus, I did. About five weeks later he came to the office to see me. At the top of the same stairs and in tears he threw his arms around me with a sobbing, "thank ya." Perhaps it was the same tone of gratitude as in the car, without the influence of alcohol. Often, I think of Patty and wonder. You never know!

"Go on," Jesus requests. "I am sure it will be helpful to others who are involved in or are considering the justice and charity ministry."

Jesus, I think one of his very active deployment attempts is to keep prodding. I find I am most vulnerable when I am tired.

An example would be the time I spent an entire day at a legislative hearing. I was advocating for benefits for refugees. Breakers would point out to me that there was little or no voter support on the issue. I should forget it, relax, and enjoy myself.

May I share with you, Jesus, how I have experienced great strength to detach myself from this type of temptation? Actually, I learned it from you. When you were on the shore after your Resurrection you had breakfast with seven of your disciples. This was after what was an unsuccessful night of fishing for them, until you intervened. Remember how Peter was all revved up about how much he loved you until you challenged him to follow you. Then, he is looking over his shoulder with the question, "What about

John"? You challenged Peter. "What if I want him to remain until I come? What concern is it of yours? You follow me."[45]

"I am not sure that I understand how you relate this to some form of evil trickery," Jesus inquires.

From the very beginning of my ministry in social justice I have continually invited individuals to join us as another voice for change on a multitude of issues that are contrary to your teachings—to the teachings of your Church. This jerk Breakers, and I frequently call him directly by this noun, tries to entice me with the available comfortable life styles versus the suffering that goes with taking a public position that is counter to our culture, perhaps even from some of my own relatives.

Jesus then asks, "Before you go on to the suggested detachments for my church and the world at large, are there any other ways that the evil one works on you"?

These would come to mind quickly. I might say the three P's: Power, Prestige, Possessions. Anyone of them can be a trap and should be targets for detachment.

"How can they trap a person"? Jesus inquires.

First, let's look at power, the struggle to control the poor. I was called to serve, versus giving them the freedom to make the final choice, would be one way of controlling the poor. Patty was given the chance to make his own choice towards recovery. The struggle to be the power filled voice for legislative actions that have a direct relationship to the quality of life of the poor should not exclude their presence, their voices and all of their power.

The suggestion of Breakers would go something like this: They are not capable of making sound decisions on their own, even after you have led them through some considerations. After all, you have the expertise. You make the decisions for them.

Again it is Breakers with: Don't bother inviting them to be with you at the hearing. You have the years of contacts and experi-

....

45 John 21:20-23

ence. They don't know how to speak. You do. Go without them. Besides, there isn't any time. Or, they got into this mess on their own, let them get out of it the same way.

Jesus asks; "Bill, what would the second P be"?

The second P would be Prestige—the temptation to glory in all the praise that comes upon you for your personal efforts in the name of charity and justice without a single ounce of recognition of your call and your grace as the sacred energy behind it all. Without me, you can do nothing.[46]

This is one of the Breakers curve balls: Stay away from too much prayer time. Your work is your prayer and there is so much to be done. Keep working and take your bows. Let everyone see how great you are.

Jesus asks, "Bill, what about the third P"?

Jesus, it is Possessions—the temptation to be careful concerning the amount of time and energy given to the social justice ministry at the expense of the attainment of material things that in the bottom line reality are only surplus.

This is the Breakers slider: You did your bit for the cause. You gave the poor family the turkey at Thanksgiving and the toys for Christmas. Take care of yourself the rest of the year.

Or: We don't want "them" here in our country. "They" will take our jobs away.

Or: Watch television. Bring up the Internet on your computer. I will show you what product you should have, the entertainment you should enjoy, how to become somebody.

Jesus then asks: "Bill, do you think your nemesis Breakers works on the Church by trying to interfere with your ministry"?

Jesus, do I think? I am certain he does. It is similar in many ways to the personal attacks. It can be very subtle or tricky and particularly anything that is divisive. You should know, Jesus, it is twenty-four hour duty watches in the battle with him. It wasn't

....

46 Ibid. page 104

long after your encounter with him in the desert that he got through to the people in the synagogue. He led them into a frenzied attack on you because you reminded them of past history where God was present to non Jews in time of needs, not the chosen people.[47]

With concern, Jesus asks; "Bill, you seem so certain? It sounds like you have had some negative experiences with the Church and the world as well."

That is true. I have had some disturbing experiences. This entire effort of my testimony is about a Servant Church. It is about charity. It is about justice. It is about being a voice for change in every situation, without exception, where people are hurting and where their God given human dignity is denied. Recently, there was a news release out of Vatican City where John Paul II challenged the laity. I think the same fundamental questions should be asked of everyone in the church:

- Have I a deep and full commitment to the Church?
- Am I faithful in my decisions to the Truth offered by the Magisterium of the church?
- Is my life permeated with the teaching of Christ's?
- Is my commitment to society and politics rooted in Gospel principles and in the social doctrine of the Church?
- What is my contribution to the enculturation of the Gospel?

At the same time I should recognize that these questions will put Breakers on the prowl again. If the truth be told, we all lack the generosity of the spirit within us at times. I can succumb to Breakers and become mean-spirited and even aggressive toward others within the Church as well as with others who are outside.

Jesus asks, "What is it, Bill, that you would advise in how to address the problem, particularly if it is something that stands in

....

47 Luke 4:25-30

the way of your inner circle leadership collaboratively participating to the fullest in the social justice mission"?

Well Jesus, we have to put a number of negative experiences out on the table in a spirit of detachment from the things that stand in the way. By so doing, there might even be a recognition of a negative posture for the first time. Here are a few detachments for consideration by the Church.

- from making personal ambitions a top priority over what is right for the mission.
- from allowing personality conflicts to interfere with healthy development.
- from words or actions that deliberately hurt or wound another, be it bishop, priest, deacon, religious or lay person.
- from being seen as part of an institution, a bureaucracy, an agency, rather than a Christ-like lifestyle.
- from public bashings of the Church, Church leaders and/or Church agencies.
- from identifying a social justice homily as too political.
- from limiting quality time for healthy discussion around the social justice doctrine and teachings of the Church.
- from taking positions on subjects based on hearing only one side.
- from behavioral patterns within the inner circle that may not always be Eucharistic.

As to the world, here are a few of many considerations for detachment:

- from stereotyping the many dedicated individuals who work untiringly for Justice and Peace as a bunch of radicals.
- from postures that are contrary to the justice we teach, be it in the area of finance, work schedules or benefits.
- from too much influence by the voices of the well meaning corporate world at the expense of justice.
- from limiting access to services at the expense of those in need.

- from an over abundance of indulgences in the use of time in a world of breathtaking technology at the expense of some time spent in silence.
- from isolating oneself from the true picture of the poverty of one kind or another that is in the community.

Jesus replies. "We still have a ways to go in your testimony Bill, so I would recommend that we leave the vineyard and meet in the morning in Greenport. Perhaps, so we don't leave on a negative note, you could close on a more encouraging one."

Yes, Jesus, hopefully some people will find this story inspiring. Gus is my oldest and dearest friend. He is one day younger than I. He spent his life in sports, both as a one hundred and thirty-five-pound running back in college football and coaching at the high school and college level. His career was closed out as a college director of athletics. His record and his age called for a well-deserved retirement to fun and games. But, fate interfered. His wife, Jane, became a stroke victim, confined to a wheelchair for the rest of her life, a life that has just ended. For fifteen years Gus provided day and night compassionate custodial care, and love, seven days a week and not without his own physical pain. In this day and age with all the controversy surrounding marriage, healthcare, and the quality of life, Gus has been an inspiration to so many. When we look for the saints of this century, don't look for those who preach or write about charity and justice. Look for the Gus's and the Jane's who patiently suffer for so long a period of time.

"Bill, give some reflection time to this question. Can a college director of athletics live in the 21st century just as I lived"?

1 John 2:5-6

CHAPTER 9

ATTACHMENT

I have told you this while I am with you. The advocate, the Holy Spirit that the Father will send in my name, he will teach you everything and remind you of all that I told you. Peace I leave with you; my peace I give to you. Not as the world gives do I give it to you. Do not let your hearts be troubled or afraid you heard me tell you, I am going away and I will come back to you. If you loved me, you would rejoice that I am going to the Father, for the Father is greater than I am. And now that I have told you this before it happens, you may believe. I will no longer speak much with you, for the ruler of the world is coming. He has no power over me, but the world must know that I love the Father and that I do just as the Father has commanded me. Get up, let us go.

John 14:25-31

Although it is shortly after dawn, a large crowd has gathered on the shoreline in Greenport. Jesus gets into a Boston Whaler and moves out a short distance.

Jesus, I would like to center this section of my testimony around love. That should be the attachment, an attachment of love for:

The Trinity—Father, Son and Spirit

The Word you brought down to us—the social teachings and doctrine

The opportunity to touch the pain of the poor.

I might call it the three T's to help our focus, Trinity—Teachings—Touch.

Jesus, full of energy asks me, "Bill, that is a fine choice. You cannot do any better. Do you remember the prayer of another one of my Jesuit brothers, Pedro Arrupe,[48] about love"?

Yes, Jesus. I do.

"Then, it might be helpful to share it at this time."

That is a good suggestion, Jesus. I think it went something like this:

> *Nothing is more practical than finding God, that is, falling in love in a quite absolute way.*
>
> *What you are in love with, what seizes your imagination will affect everything.*
>
> *It will decide:*
> *What time you will get out of bed in the morning*
> *What you will do with your evenings*
> *How you will spend your weekends*
> *What you read*
> *Who you know*
> *What breaks your heart*
> *What amazes you with joy and gratitude*

Jesus seems very pleased in hearing it again. "Go on, Bill."

Jesus, I am trying to establish a blueprint for our brothers and sisters to become well grounded in social justice as a ministry. At the same time, I am striving to avoid becoming a secular humanist. This is not only challenging but also very uplifting. It is God's work. I need to develop with God's grace into a deep, fire in the belly Trinitarian love. Unlike the no trespassing pre-Vatican Council days I am called by you to go headfirst into the mystery that you

....

48 Deceased Provincial of the Society of Jesus.

taught us in the second sentence of the above scripture passage. What is it, Jesus, that you told us? Tell us again. Some of us are slow learners.

Jesus replies. "The proof of the love of me rests in your attachment to my words, my teachings, and the teachings of the Spirit who came after me as I promised. If you do, my Father will love you and we will develop an intimate relationship with you. It may help if you visualize a never-ending line of a circle: Father-Son-Spirit-You, and the person in pain."

I believe, Jesus, that is the reason you led me to the Listening Prayer as the first step in building the foundation for involvement in the justice mission, as well as the second step of Detachment.

Jesus continues to teach. "Yes, Bill, that is true. As I mentioned, I give you a love, a peace that you will not find from the world. But, you have to listen to my teachings with a clear heart. If your heart is cluttered with worldly troubles, fears and anxieties you cannot hear me. You cannot be conscious that you are the recipient of the Divine love nor can that love be reciprocal with the Trinity, with my teachings and with those in pain."

I am beginning to understand, Jesus.

"Bill, what has been your experience with the Trinitarian love"? Jesus asks me.

Jesus, sometimes images help particularly when one is dealing with the subject of Fatherly love. Patrick is a two year old grandson who was born prematurely and had a struggle to live due to an underdeveloped body. Thanks to God, today Patrick is a healthy, young child. There was a snapshot taken of him in my arms, which I have on my desk where Patrick stares at me through the spokes of a letter holder. Well, Jesus, you know this scenario helps me with a great sense of the Father and his love, particularly his love for those who are involved in a struggle of one kind or another. He holds us, each and every one of us, in his arms with care and affection. That photograph symbolizes for me, and I hope for everyone, the love of the Father that you so often referred to when you were here. Patrick has two sisters, Erin and Michael, who had similar experiences. Today, they are healthy children in elementary school. Lest the other eighteen grandchildren get their noses out of joint, I have the same setting in snapshots of you with me.

Back in 1948 I left home at 7:30 A.M. to go to work. My wife was in the seventh month of what appeared to be a normal pregnancy. In those years we didn't have the advanced medical technology of today to determine the gender. When I arrived at my office there was a message to call home. In the short space of the travel time of one hour my wife was in the hospital and in the hands of her obstetrician. At 10:30 A.M. on April Fool's Day I was greeted by Dr. Charles with, "Congratulations, you are the father of twin girls—three pounds and five pounds respectively." Well, Mary, the stronger of the two, survived only one day. Janet struggled for life for a month. Today, Janet has raised three children and guides hundreds of others as a grade school teacher. Oh, how many the opportunities to be fused to the Trinitarian love. Oh, how the contemporary pro choice culture destroys affection of parents for their children and children for their parents. Another image is when Angela or I would cover one of our children with a blanket that they kicked off on a cold, winter night. How well that images the love the Father has for each one of his six billion children that He covers every night.

Jesus responds: "What a beautiful image. Men and women show their love for the Father in so many ways—in private prayer—in Church—in community with a liturgy. In your travels did you ever experience or witness love for the Father in other ways"?

Yes, Jesus, I did. When I was traveling around the country to conferences about the Social Justice Doctrine and Teachings of the Church I befriended Lion, a Native American. Now, we were both early risers and enjoyed a 5:00 A.M. walk. I would go to early morning Eucharist. Lion would go off to the highest place he could find. In a country setting that would be the top of a hill. In the big cities it would be the roof of a high rise hotel. From that place Lion would watch the sun rise as he worshipped and loved the Father. I am sure the Father looked down with the same love on this man who was preserving the customs that were taught to him by his father and grandfather.

"Is the Trinity becoming less of a mystery, Bill"? Jesus inquires.

In my mind, Jesus, no. In my heart, yes.

"Bill, do you have any other thoughts or stories relating to the Trinitarian love"?

I do Jesus, and I would like to share them with you. You know to this day I cannot comprehend how any man, woman or child who has reached the age of reason can look up at you on the Cross without having a passionate love for you, for your Father who willed it and for your Spirit who breathes within us. You suffered an indescribable pain and agony to atone for our sins. How can anyone who seriously reflects on this truth not overflow with a passionate love for you.

There is another story that may help in understanding this concern of mine. There was a time during World War II when I was training to be a pilot. In my platoon there was an obnoxious cadet whom nobody could tolerate. God, forgive me. There was one exercise that we all dreaded. Fully clothed and with a full pack I had to swim fifty feet in fifteen feet of water. Our platoon's schedule called for a 3:00 P.M. exercise. Not only did I worry all morning, but by 3:00 P.M. the fear became a reality as the packs were well soaked from the earlier platoons. Well, Jesus, I jumped in at the signal and half way across I am reflecting as to what all the worry was about. This was a breeze. As I stopped treading water to congratulate myself, I began to sink. From under the surface I could see the wrinkled faces of my instructor and fellow cadets. But, no one is reacting to help me in my distress. There was one exception. It was Horace, the obnoxious cadet. He jumped into the water and removed the pack as I surfaced to breathe the fresh, dry air that I needed. Obviously, I haven't forgotten the incident nor will I forget what Horace did for me. It is the same logic that I use when I think about what you did for me, Jesus. Why did it take so long for me to recognize your great sacrifice? Why did it take so long to love? Why isn't the crucifixion the headlines of our newspapers? Why isn't the suffering of those three hours the feature report on the evening news? Why isn't the agony of the atonement for our sins the priority of the Internet? This is the marketing I referred to in an earlier part of my testimony.

Soul of Christ be my sanctification
Body of Christ be my salvation
Blood of Christ fill all my veins
Water of Christ's side wash out my stains
Passion of Christ my comfort be
Oh good Jesus listen to me
In thy wounds I fain would hide
Never to be parted from your side.

Jesus asks, "A beautiful tribute, who wrote it"? I think it was St. Ignatius Loyola. This is why I must begin the growth process in the Church's social justice ministry at the foot of the Cross. Let every minute of those three hours saturate every ounce of my being, every ounce of my body and soul, and, in the spirit of complete nakedness of my soul, I too cry out: "My God, my God, why have you forsaken me"? Now, I am ready for the transition from the nakedness of my soul to a fullness. It is a fullness that enables me to believe in those words of yours and the Father at the Last Supper when you promised the disciples that the Father would send the Holy Spirit in my name to remind you and teach you as I have taught you.[49]

"Bill, you now seem to have a sense in all of its oneness of the love of the Trinity. Do you think that this is a good beginning for anyone with a serious commitment to be my disciple and especially one who wants to work for systemic change to lighten the burdens of the poor"? Jesus asks.

Yes, I do. You know, Jesus, John XXIII, early on in his papacy, had some profound advice for himself and for us on the subject of

....

49 John 14:26

addressing the weighty problems of the world. He said that "if you don't remain a disciple of the gentle and humble Master you will understand nothing, even of temporal realities. Then, you will be really blind."

After these seventeen years of direct involvement in the vocation of charity and justice, I am convinced that the weakness of the justice movement, in the truest sense of the term, comes from a lack of understanding and commitment to discipleship. Again, at the risk of repetition, I have to find quality time in prayer and in developing a relationship with you, Jesus. True discipleship means living just as you lived. Then, I will be empowered to believe in the great God given gift of love. I will believe in the love of the Father. I will believe in your love, Jesus. I will believe in the love of the Spirit within me. I will believe that this love has always been there but too often I am a victim of ignorance. Then, it will be in faith that I will not only enhance the great works of charity, but I will also link my faith to justice with the oneness of the Trinitarian love.

"Bill, why don't we go on now. You mention that the subject of Attachment would have three objects which you call the three T's." Jesus requests.

Well Jesus, I hope this testimony produces a better vision of the Trinitarian love than I experienced in the era of the pre-second Vatican Council. The people on the beach seem to be having a better vision of the Trinitarian love as well.

Jesus prompts me. "I believe you were about to address an attachment of love for my teachings, in particular my teachings and my activities around justice."

Yes Jesus, I should also include how this is a perfect fit into the never ending line of the occupants of the circle. As I keep emphasizing, one of the major obstacles in addressing the multitude of the causes of injustices which are swallowing us up in communities, in our nation and globally, rests with lack of theological education. When the clergy admit that there is a void in their own social justice education which does not enable them to preach, teach and serve and when the laity complain that they haven't heard the message, there is an obvious problem. Jesus, how can they be expected to touch the pain of the poor and love them with your love if such a lack of education exists?

Jesus asks. "Bill, would you speak to the specific flow of the curriculum that seems to reach people? What is it that they are not hearing"?

Jesus, the flow that I mentioned comes from a combination of your teachings by Father Bryan Hehir[50] and the Woodstock Theological Center at Georgetown University. The flow is what one would expect. It begins with:

- Genesis, creation, the dignity of the person, am I my brother's keeper, care of the environment.
- Then, to the prophets and justice, judgment of society as to how women, widows, children, orphans, aliens and refugees are treated.
- The New Testament—your prayer life, Jesus, your relationship to the Father—your hands on experience with the people of your time on earth—healing—confrontation with the authorities where there was injustice.
- One hundred and eight Years of Catholic Social Doctrine and Teachings beginning with Pope Leo XIII and on to John Paul II
- Bishops' Pastorals on issues of life, economic justice, discrimination and violence.

Does that give you a picture of what people say they are not hearing, Jesus?

"Yes, it does. Finish up with your third attachment thought about touching the pain."

Jesus, you know as well as I do that if I don't know what hurts people, how can I love them. I become attached to them by touching the pain where they are. Liturgical and/or private prayers for the poor are good but they also call for the one on one personal

....

50 Advisor to the U.S. Bishops Conference, Dean Harvard School of Divinity

contact with your compassion. I need both. It is not only a grace filled experience for them but also for me.

Jesus suggests: "Why don't you share some of your other personal experiences of touching the pain of others, perhaps in the early years in your own parish. community."

Jesus, as you know, you blessed me with a very special gift, among so many. That was the privilege of carrying your sacred body in the Eucharist to the patients at Little Flower Nursing Home for eight years. I cannot enter fully into the national justice debate around Medicare, Medicaid, and Social Security without the experience of touching the pain of the elderly and touching the pain of the nursing home patients with a one on one contact. Then, oh, how love fills and flows from your veins. Jesus, you suggested earlier that I am engaged in heavy lifting so I need at times a lighter touch with a little humor. During those nursing home visits often I would be asked, "Are you a Father"? That was a pre-Vatican Council mentality that this sacred function had to be performed by a priest. I would respond, "yes, I am a father, a father of eight children." There was another time that one of the patients, an eighty-nine year old woman who was blind and totally confined to a wheelchair or bed, startled me with a comment that she could not receive the Eucharist. I expressed my concern with "Why Edith"? "Because I had impure thoughts during the night." You handle that one, Jesus.

"Bill, do you find it disturbing when individuals walk away from the pain, particularly of the elderly when they are lonely or ill".?

Yes Jesus, it brings me back to the Acts of the Apostles and how the outer circle would witness the behavioral patterns of the inner circle of the early Christians with "see how they love one another."[51] I may never know what influence my one act of

....

51 Early Christian Writings

charity and/or justice has on individuals outside the circle. It reminds me of an incident twenty-seven years ago. In my role as general manager of a retail store I was out on an observation tour of the selling floor when my bell page was calling me. When I contacted the operator she informed me that I had a long distance call. Now, Jesus, it had been seventeen years since I had left Mindanao in the southernmost part of the Philippine Islands just prior to the end of the war. It had been seventeen years since I had seen or heard from any of the other pilots. Now, I heard the voice of Tom in his best southern, Georgia drawl. He had a friend, more than a friend, an adopted father who brought all kinds of support to Tom in the post war period. Tom senior was going to Boston for serious stomach surgery at the Leahy Clinic. Would I make contact with him and bring our presence to him in anyway there was a need. Angela and I made the contact the following day and for the next thirty days after the surgery. I, really Angela, tried to bring love and practical care to him. We tried to take the place of his relatives and friends back in Georgia. Jesus, Tom was a southern Baptist. When he was leaving our home to return to Georgia he concluded his expressions of gratitude with this comment. "Are you sure you both are Catholics? I cannot believe what you have done for me, a Baptist." It proves that as a Catholic, I too, am sometimes stereotyped. But, it also proves that when I am detached from the obstacles that stand in my way, I will hear so many invitations to be attached to the pain of the other Toms of the world as they say: "See how I am loved."

"Bill, it is stories like that, which do so much for the conversion of hearts and lead people to involvement, not only in acts of charity, as was your story of the fine Georgian gentleman, but to address the causes of injustice and bring about change."

"Did you ever hear from him again, Bill"? Jesus asks.

Yes, every Christmas we received a box of Georgian pecans with a nice note.

You know, Jesus, there are so many wonderful people in all of our parish communities who are involved in the St. Vincent de

Paul Mission and Parish Social Ministry. Yet, in any one parish, the range can run from twelve to, in some cases, two to three hundred. That would be the tops. This is what I referred to earlier as a gatekeeper mentality. At the highest level of the curve it is a very small percentage of the total active parishioners. It is a minute percentage of the total of inactive Catholics who are visible only at Christmas and Easter. When you move into the area of active involvement in being a strong voice for justice in this world of so much disrespect for life from the womb to the tomb, I find the percentage of activity in any one parish community drops to an alarmingly low level. Disrespect for life can take many forms: street violence, discrimination, religious prejudice, and persecution, and indifference to the pain around us. Obviously, in this large population, the people are over and over again telling us they are not hearing your gospel message as it relates to the signs of the times in which we live. But, when they hear your justice message in a prayerful climate, they are energized to be a part of the mission. I must keep this testimony focused, repeatedly, on the truth of these experiences. This is the challenge to your disciples in the next millennium.

"You must have some thoughts, Bill, as to what you would ask people to prayerfully consider."

I do, Jesus, and I will. But first, I would like to conclude this third T, touching the pain, with an observation and four other related stories. Sometimes people will say "they" are doing a great job. They don't need anymore help. Besides, I don't have anything to contribute. Wrong—wrong—wrong on all three counts. If all of the pain of a community were surfaced, every last individual in the community wouldn't be sufficient to respond. The hurting and the healthy individuals have to see how we love one another and then they will come to us. Everyone has some gift to share in the community. It may be as simple as bartering two hours of television for one hour of listening prayer and one hour in advocating for a Social Security Benefit that provides for the rock bottom basic necessities of life for a seventy-eight year old widow who has no other income.

Jesus seems to ponder, "Bill, do you remember the woman

who was evicted from the home by her own son and daughter-in-law? She happened to be seventy-eight also."

How could I ever forget it, Jesus. It seems like it was yesterday when I drove up to the house with the outreach volunteer who was sharing her gift as a professional real estate broker. What a sorrowful picture it was. The sidewalk cluttered with the personal belongings of this elderly woman, in the presence of the sheriff to insure the execution of the court ordered eviction. It was a moving experience for me. Without going into details, how can such a tragedy occur in the middle of a Christian community on a middle America street? The compassionate real estate broker had some practical assistance to offer the now homeless woman. The presence of the Church in an expression of love was an indescribable support to the evicted woman. Some time, somewhere, prayerfully it will be an example to other sons, daughters, their spouses, of another way, your way, Jesus.

From the stern, Jesus asks: "Bill, that was another good example of a Servant Church. Do people that have been helped, either through material assistance or through your advocacy to change laws that unjustly bind them, ever come back to express a word of gratitude"?

Often they do, Jesus. Sometimes they come back and share their gifts with another hurting person. Back in the parish days there was a crippled man who over a period of probably three to four years would come regularly for food, occasionally for partial rent assistance and most of all for companionship as he lived alone in a single room. His SSI benefit just was not sufficient to cover the basic needs of food, rent and utilities. The volunteers of St. Vincent de Paul and the Outreach provided the support. I can remember times when I would see him struggling with his steps as he came across the parking lot. I would say to myself, "Not again, not today anyway." I lost track of him for many years. One Christmas I received a card from him from another state. Enclosed was a picture of his wife and infant daughter with a greeting, "To Bill—Have a wonderful Christmas and a great New Year. From all of us to you." Jesus, as they say in the state lottery advertisement—You never know—you just never know.

"Why doesn't the community or the neighbors see and respond to some of these situations"? Jesus asks me.

I think sometimes it is out of fear. Maybe other times it is out of haughtiness. I repeat, I believe the answer rests in the education and training. People have to hear the theological foundations of why they have a responsibility to respond in charity and justice. They have to be lead back to you on the Cross.

"Will there be any faith on earth when I return"?[52] Jesus asks again as he closes his eyes and directs the question towards the listening crowd on this Greenport Beach.

Jesus, I really believe there will be. You know there is a hidden hunger for something else beyond the experience of today's culture. Most are not sure what it is. People on both sides of the spectrum, those who believe that we don't have any poor in our community and those who share their baptismal gifts with them, always seem to find you in this relationship. The challenge for the next millennium is to expand the base. The need is for more and more trained individuals to go to the foot of the Cross and then out to touch the pain with the poor wherever they are.

"Are there any examples of injustices in a small community such as Greenport? If so, what can be done about them"? Jesus continues his questions.

There are two that come to mind quickly. One was of a welfare mother and two small children, a boy and a girl, six and eight, who were placed in a house by the Social Service Department. On the front door was a notice from the town health department citing eighteen violations. It is incongruous that in that day and age or this day and age that individuals dependent on their government to help them through a crisis could be asked to live in these sub-standard conditions. What can be done about it? The voices of the communities

....

52 Luke 18:8

should be heard. Remember, earlier in my testimony, the senator's challenge—"politics is a game of numbers."

The other story is again on a street in the heart of middle America. It is a family of four. There was a permanently disabled father with arthritis and the mother who cares for a twelve-year old autistic son and a school age teen. They lived in sub-standard housing with their only income from social Security and SSI. The father would get his fresh air and recreation in good weather by making a difficult trip from the house to an old, disabled car in the dirt driveway. The autistic child who at times was capable of violence to self or to others was under the watchful eyes and attention of the mother, twenty-four hours a day, seven days a week. What can be done about it? First and foremost, the neighbors could tear down the isolation walls and bring a friendly smile, a hot meal, and an occasional laugh. Professionally, it would be helpful to advocate for care of the autistic child. We have experienced some wonderful, parish social ministries in our communities. Once thirty dedicated volunteers started a hospice for the parish community. This was not a Catholic thing but for everyone. There is a need for creativity and imagination, Jesus, in order to witness your teachings. Why not a hospice for autistic children and their parents. So, you see, Jesus, we need not three hundred but three thousand community members doing something, no matter how small it may be. This is the attachment that I should seek. It is the attachment of the Trinitarian love within me fused to the pain of my neighbor and to solutions that will free them from that pain. These stories are all examples of the development process of building truly Christian compassionate communities as the body of Christ—Baptist, Lutheran, Episcopalian, Methodist, Hindu, Jew, Muslin, agnostic, atheist, Catholic—ONE.

Jesus brings these thoughts to a conclusion with his ongoing challenging question as I pull up the anchor.

"Can a housewife live in the twenty-first century just as I lived"?

1 John 2:5-6

CHAPTER 10

BLESSED

And great crowds from Galilee, the Decapolis, Jerusalem and Judea and from beyond the Jordan followed him. When he saw the crowds he went up the mountain and after he sat down, his disciples came to him. He began to teach them.

Matthew 4:25 5:1-2

"Bill, we have a full day ahead of us as I am going to teach the Beatitudes."

Jesus, before I listen to them I have a couple of questions. It is so easy for me to again treat all this as a mere narrative from two thousand years ago. How do I avoid this trap?

"Before you open your heart to my teachings why don't you reflect on the home location of my listeners," Jesus responds as an answer to my concern.

Do you mean, Jesus, you are to speak to great crowds that are gathered here again on a hillside in Fort Salonga? They come from Elmont, Floral Park, Hempstead, Rockville Centre, Smithtown, Brentwood and Riverhead, and beyond to the North and South Forks of Long Island?

"Yes, Bill. What is the other question"? Jesus displays alertness to the reference of a couple of questions.

Isn't there another challenge beyond the narrative problem, namely to change hearts to conformance with your teachings and your will?

"Yes and that is not as easy as changing the geography. Why don't you share the hunter's story?[53] It may help with the focus on change."

It is one of my favorite stories. It is a surprise to me that you were aware of it. Two men chartered a plane out in East Hampton to take them up into the wilds of Canada to hunt deer. After they landed on the dirt airstrip they unloaded their belongings with the mutual understanding that the pilot would be back in a week to take them back to Long Island. When the plane returned at the appointed time, the pilot noticed, as he taxied up to where the men were standing, two dead deer on the ground. When he got out of the plane he surprised the men with this comment: "There is no way that this plane can handle both of you, your luggage and the two deer."

"Well, last year we shot two deer and the pilot said it would be okay." One of the men replied.

"All right then, if the pilot said it would be okay last year we will do it the same way this year. Load up and we will get moving," said the pilot.

The loaded plane taxied to the end of the strip, turned around and proceeded to take off. About three miles off the end of the strip the plane lost its power and crashed. The two hunters crawled out of the wreckage and one man said to the other, "Do you have any idea where we are?" The other replied, "I think we are about one mile east of where we crashed last year."

Jesus comments; "That is a great story. Why do you repeat it so often"?

There is a great lesson to be learned from it. The world is crowded with last year-itis, in the corporate world, in the Church and in our own personal, behavioral patterns. I end up with little or no progress as I keep repeating the same ways I did it last year. This is especially true of my mistakes. When I am locked into this pattern I am not leaving any room for my imagination to roam or to let my creative juices flow. Could I now move on to your teachings with the great crowds, only now it is to a different crowd in a different contemporary location.

Jesus comments; "How true, Bill. You need to put the new

wine into new barrels. Maybe, the new wine is the Catholic Social Justice Teachings. New in the sense that as you have said a number of times before, people are not hearing my message, particularly around justice."

Go on then, Jesus, with your teachings to the great crowd, only not in your time on earth, but to the great crowd of our day. Maybe, I can apply your lessons to some of the injustices I identified in the thirty day vigil of injustices. This covered close to three hundred headlines and two hundred-ninety-eight thousand lines of copy, as a decent sample of the signs of the times in January, 1999 published in the New York Times.

Jesus begins,

> *"Blessed are the poor in spirit,*
> *For theirs is the kingdom of heaven."*

Jesus, are you addressing the anawim of the Old Testament—those people who were without material possessions but who had complete confidence in God?

"No, it is a broader group. I wanted to extend the blessing to all—whatever step of the social ladder they are on and in the spirit of poverty they are very much aware of their dependence on God."

Jesus continues, again without any comments from me about the headlines;

> *"Blessed are the meek for they will inherit the land."*

News Headlines:

- Suit Filed—Two Hundred and Seventy Thousand Acres Unlawfully acquired from Native Americans.
- Unconstitutional Racial Gerrymander Discriminates Against Blacks.
- Congo's Struggle May Unleash Broad Strife To Redraw Africa.

....

53 deMello, S.J., Anthony Taking Flight

There doesn't seem to be any shortage of issues that have to do with the acquisitions of land. Please go on, Jesus.

"Blessed are they who hunger and thirst for Righteousness for they will be satisfied."

News Headlines:
- Agriculture Department To Settle Lawsuit By Black Farmers
- Despite Billions Spent On School Buildings, A History Of Failures
- One Hundred Thousand Abortion Opponents Parade Past The White House.

Jesus, another of the news headlines reads:
- Dispute Over Financing Stalls Housing For The Mentally Ill Homeless
- Seeing How Poor People Really Live Instead Of Sitting And Watching A Video
- One Hundred And Thirty Million Indonesians Live In Poverty
- New York City Admits Turning Away The Poor
- New York Lawsuits Say Unscrupulous Lending Is Taking Homes From The Poor

Jesus, nor is there any shortage of issues around righteousness.

Jesus continues again without any reference to the headlines. Does he prefer some reflection time in silence?

"Blessed are they who mourn for they will be comforted."

News Headline:
- Missile Misfire Kills Eleven Civilians
- Black Man Murdered By White Supremists
- Twelve Americans Die in Embassy Bombings
- 2,768 People Killed In Fighting in Sierra Leone

Jesus continues his comments on mercy.

"Blessed are the merciful for they will be shown mercy."

News Headlines: (continue from the Thirty Day Vigil on Injustices)
- Moved by Pope, Governor Commutes Death Sentence
- Pope Urges U.S. Catholics To Oppose Death Penalty

Jesus continues, as the crowd becomes uneasy with the message.

"Blessed are the clean of heart for they will see God."

Do you think, Jesus, that this promise for eternity will bring about some conversions of hearts?

"Well, Bill, it is a promise I made two thousand years ago and it is still valid today. Only if they will listen, only if they will apply it to the signs of the times of today. May I go on"?

"Blessed are the peacemakers for they will be called children of God."

News Headlines:
- Colombian Town Gropes For A Peace Of Its Own
- U.S. Ready To Ease Some Restrictions In Policy On Cuba
- President Sends Ambassador To Kosovo To Discuss Peace Terms

Jesus concludes:

"Blessed are they who are persecuted for the sake of righteousness for theirs is the kingdom of heaven."

News Headline:
- The World Expected Peace. It Found A New Brutality.

The Stories:

- Babies die of cold on hillsides where mothers have fled to save their lives in Kosovo.
- Madmen cut off the hands of teenage boys in Sierra Leone.
- Relief planes are shot down in Angola.
- The United Nations drifts without policy decision regarding the economic sanctions of Iraq while thousands suffer and die due to lack of needed medicine and food.
- Chaos has returned to the poorest nation in the world—Haiti.
- Crimes against humanity are shielded in a number of countries from international inspections.

Jesus recalls a famous quote by General Omar Bradley: "We have grasped the mystery of the atom and we have rejected the Sermon on the Mount." After a few minutes of silence, Jesus continues. "Bill, where do you suggest we go from here"?

It has been a long day, Jesus. The people are tired, physically and mentally. Let them go home and rest until morning. Would you leave them with a question for their prayerful reflection?

"I am happy to do so." Jesus turns to the crowd and says, "Would each one of you reflect on how you can bring the blessings of the Beatitudes to a reality in the twenty first century."

CHAPTER 11

CHURCH[54]

In the beginning was the Word and the Word was with God and the Word was God.

He was in the beginning with God.

All things came to be through him, and without him nothing came to be.

What came to be through him was life, and this life was the light of the human race; the light shines in the darkness, and the darkness has not overcome it.

John 1: 1-5

"Bill, you and the crowd appear to be rested after the long day yesterday. Where would you like to begin this morning"?

Jesus, I would like to begin to spend some time on three documents of the Second Vatican Council. These inspired teachings are central to the Social Justice Mission.

"What would they be"? Jesus asks.

I need a better and clearer understanding of the Church and the roles of the Church and the laity in the reality of today's world.

"That is some assignment. Let's get at it. Why don't we start with the Church? Bill, you kick it off ," as his face transmits rays of enthusiasm.

You will recall how early on in my testimony I referred to the

....

54 II Vatican Council, Dogmatic Constitution on the Church, Lumen Gentium, 21 November 1964

prayerful question of John XXIII prior to the Council convening. “The Church should be a Beacon of Light—what should that exemplary light be”? Jesus, why not start there?

Jesus replies in a voice that everyone in the great crowd that had come from the Queens line to the tips of the forks on the East End can hear:

> *“I am the Light of all humanity and I shine out visibly from the Church.”*

Jesus continues to challenge everyone, “You can no longer live in privacy or isolated as you are being drawn together socially and culturally. Modern technology, which you have developed, has removed any and all global barriers. My dear brothers and sisters, you should also remember how the headlines we just reviewed came from around the world to you in your daily newspapers or into your living room through the television. Yet, are you still a long way from full unity with me? Yes. Even within the institutional Church is there not a long way to go? Even within your nuclear families, full unity with me is attainable but a distance remains.”

Jesus, it is exactly for that reason that you are the Light of all Humanity that I recommend that before anyone starts out on the journey to justice, they go to the foot of the Cross.

“Bill, this is where I want them to begin. I call every man, woman and child to a union with me. I call them to direct their lives to me as the blood and water flowed from my side, for them and for all victims of injustice.”

Jesus, when I began my testimony and a number of other times I refer to the Servant Church. Am I on the right track?

Jesus directs his answer in a loud voice to the crowds: “You have all heard me say that I came to serve and to give my life as a ransom for many.[55] The identification of the Servant Church tells

....

55 Mark 10:45

it all. You, the people of Long Island, and people everywhere, are that Church. You, too, are called to serve one another. You are called to give a priority to your lives with my teachings and the social justice teachings of my Church as your foundation. I have not called you to exchange the comforts of your suburban lifestyles for death as I have in other parts of the world. Think back for a moment to some of the headlines we addressed yesterday."

Jesus, often we find ourselves in the we/they climate. Sometimes, it can result in discrimination. Help us with this one.

"In my human nature I overcame death through my own death and resurrection. I redeemed every person, regardless of their race, their color or their creed. By so doing I changed them. They have become the builders of the foundation for change. I changed them into a new creation."[56] Jesus replies.

A person from Rockville Centre speaks up. "Jesus, it is very difficult at times to go out and touch the pain of a neighbor in Hempstead. What will help me to be more open"?

"I didn't get your name." Jesus asks.

"Martin."

"You have to be open to the Spirit within you. The Spirit will produce and stimulate the love, not only for you Martin, but also for all of the faithful gathered here on this hill in Fort Salonga. You asked how to be more open. You are also wondering why should you have the concern in the first place," as Jesus reads Martin's concerns.

"Jesus, you read my innermost thoughts. I have enough problems of my own." Martin replies.

"Martin, if one member of my Mystical Body suffers, all the parts suffer with it; if one part is honored, all the parts share its joy."[57]

Martin smiles. "Jesus, maybe you are giving us a clue to the answer to the question you keep repeating at the end of each day."

....

56 Galatians 6:15; 2 Corinthians 5:17

57 1 Corinthians 12:26

"That is exactly what I am doing. I am trying to help the people who are listening to this testimony. I am trying to help those who have gathered here from other villages of Long Island. The answer to the question is that all the members must be formed in my likeness until I am formed in them.[58] You are created in my image and likeness. You are experiencing this period of living in the world with all its trials and oppressions as I experience them. You are associated with my sufferings as head of the Body—the Church. You are also called to share the pain and the sufferings of the poor before you will be called to the final glorification."

A woman from Elmont asks: "Jesus, is this not helpful in addressing the challenge we hear so often about separating matters of the state from what some people feel is not a subject for the Church, for example, the decision to have an abortion. The state has made the decision that it is my personal choice."

"I am sorry, I didn't get your name." Jesus personalizes the conversation.

"My name is Helen."

Jesus replies. "I am glad it is helpful to you Helen. I hope it will be helpful to everyone. May I do an add-on. There are three areas we cannot separate. They are:

- a society structured with hierarchical organs and my Mystical Body
- the visible society and the spiritual community
- the earthly Church and the Church endowed with heavenly riches."

Helen queries Jesus, "do you mean they are one"?

Jesus replies, "that's exactly what I mean—they are ONE. They come together with both a human and a divine element. Bill, you have a comment"?

Yes, Jesus. This being the truth, then it would seem that we need human resources to carry out the mission. This in turn sup-

....

58 Galatians 4:19

ports the need for theological education and training around charity and its direct connection to justice as a priority consideration. But, the listeners to the testimony and all men and women have to know the mission. This is not for any earthly glory but rather in total humility to witness your lifestyle.

Jesus replies, "you also have to remind everyone why I was sent down to earth by the Father. I was sent to:

- bring the Good News to the poor
- heal the contrite of heart
- seek and save what was lost
- love those afflicted by human misery

The poor and the suffering reflect me. They are the image of me. So, as you, my dear brothers and sisters, respond to their needs, you are serving for me. You have an active role in the Servant Church."

Louis, a twenty-six year old man from Greenpoint asks Jesus, "who makes up this church you mention? When I go back to my parish community in Greenpoint how will I recognize who are the members of this Church"?

The teacher continues, "Louis, we might say that the church is the new people of God, made up of Jews and Gentiles in your Greenpoint community. They are all one in spirit. I am the head. This is not a Catholic thing. It is those people of God, called by God, to share their gifts as they persevere in charity and as a voice for justice. They have to be open to my grace to make it happen. If they don't respond they are members of the Church in mind only, not in body. It is serious when they close the door to the grace that I have offered them as children of my Church."

"Sometimes, we hear that the Church is hierarchical" asks a woman named Brigid from Floral Park. "The word hierarchical is scary in and of itself, Jesus. Would you explain it to us"?

Looking first at Brigid and then out to the crowd, Jesus replies. "Brigid, when you become involved in discussions about

Church go back to the beginning. Reflect on how it all started. Remember that the Father sent me. I set up the holy Church. After lengthy communications with my Father in prayer, I entrusted the mission to the Apostles with Peter as the head."

"Jesus, where did they start with the mission"? A young teenager by the name of Joseph inquires.

Jesus replies, "Joseph was my stepfather's name. They went out to the Israelites first and then to all the people, Jew and Gentile. They took my place with a responsibility to teach in hierarchical communion with Peter as the head and the other members."

"What were they to teach the people"? Another asks.

Jesus walks out among the crowd as he continues his teaching. "It was their duty to teach the faithful about love of the whole Church, all men and women, and especially the poor, the suffering and the individuals who were persecuted for the sake of justice. That duty has been passed on down to the present which is represented in the line of succession which I established. Is it not around that teaching that the title of this testimony comes: to touch the pain of the poor, the suffering, and the persecuted for the sake of justice? So you can see my dear brothers and sisters that your involvement in charity and justice has deep roots which are both human and divine."

"Where do the priests fit into this hierarchical structure"? A priest asks.

Jesus replies with doctrinal clarity, "Priests are the representatives of the bishop in your respective, local settings. They are key. They are leaders in your communities. They use all the resources available to them under the bishop and the Pope to eliminate division and dissension in every shape and form."

"My name is Tom and I am from Floral Park. Before the crowd goes home to their communities Jesus, what about the lay people"?

"Yes, where do we fit into this hierarchical structure"? A senior from Southold asks.

In a direct challenge to anyone who desires to be a true disciple, Jesus replies, "Everything we have discussed pertains to the laity as well as the clergy, deacons and religious. As the people of God, you all share in my priestly, prophetic and kingly office. To the best of your ability you are entrusted with the responsibility to carry on with the mission as a part of the whole Christian people in the Church and out there in the world. As the people of God you are called to influence and to direct the temporal affairs of the world to God's will. As my brothers and sisters, you are called to manifest me, my lifestyle, my suffering, my death and my resurrection to other men and women. In me and in the Church there is no inequality arising from sex, race, nationality, or social condition."

"Why"? A voice from the crowd asks.

Making eye contact first with the woman who asks the question and then with the crowd, Jesus replies. "Because there is neither Jew nor Greek, neither slave nor free man, male or female, for you are all one in me, Jesus Christ.[59] Thank you for this time together. Go home now and make the Gospel shine out to the rest of your community and the world, in your daily life, in your family life and in your social life. Join your profession of faith to a life of faith. Change hearts as I have taught you."

As we walk out to my 1993 Buick a middle-aged man asks Jesus:"Can my years of being away from the hierarchical Church stand in the way of my present desire to live your lifestyle, Jesus, in the twenty-first century"?

1 John 2:5-6

....

59 Galatians 3:28; Colossians 3:11

CHAPTER 12

WORLD

> *The way we came to know love was that he laid down his life for us; so we ought to lay down our lives for our brothers/sisters. If someone who has worldly means sees a brother/sister in need and refuses him/her compassion, how can the love of God remain in him/her? Children, let us love not in word or speech but in deed and truth.*
>
> *1 John 3:17-18*

As we drive along the Long Island Expressway, Jesus appears to be totally engrossed in the newspaper reports around the atrocities in Kosovo. I interrupt.

When I began this testimony, Jesus, I identified so much hurt and pain that exist in the heart of our own communities, in our nation and throughout the world. It is a world that comes into our workplace in the daytime or the living room at night. I enjoy in both settings the fruits of our tremendous, rapid advancements in technology. Would that my knowledge, understanding and implementation of the principles of Judeo/Christian social justice have kept the same pace. I am very much aware that your bishops addressed these problems at the Second Vatican Council but at this point in time only a few of the clergy or laity seem to be aware of the justice happenings of the Council.

Jesus replies. "You are quite right, Bill. You know another one of the documents which you want to know a little more about, the

Church in the Modern World, was not on the original agenda. My father and I were very much aware of this when we prompted Cardinal Suennens to challenge his brother bishops with the question to them—'Church of Christ—what do you say for yourself'? We saw the need to go beyond the point at which the Council was at and to be more pastoral and direct the dialogue at the hurt and pain that people were experiencing as well as to challenge my Church as the people of God to respond."

How did the council respond to the challenge of Cardinal Suennens?

Jesus replies. "The preamble of the *Church in the Modern World* is my response through the instrumentality of the bishops at the Council proceedings. These are my words coming from the Sacred Heart of My Soul—then—now—forever.

'The joys and the hopes of the men and women of this age, especially the poor and the oppressed, are my joys and my hopes.'

If you wish to be my follower, they have to be yours as well. You have to listen to their cries and bring my compassionate heart to them. You have to strive to free them from the chains that bind them."

I do hear you, Jesus, and I am trying. There is such an urgent need for our brothers and sisters to hear what you are saying to us and to hear what the poor and oppressed are saying to us. Your presence, your word, and these experiences will help us. Between the lines of every news communications are the faces and voices of people who are the poor, oppressed women, children and men crying out for some type of freedom.

"What is your interpretation of the word, freedom"? Jesus asks.

A presidential candidate once described it this way. "Freedom is an indivisible word. If we want to enjoy it and fight for it we must be prepared to extend it to everyone whether they are rich or poor, whether they are with us or not, no matter what their race or the color of their skin."[60]

....

60 Wilkie, Wendell, Presidential Candidate, 1942

Jesus, there was a recent news item that had to do with the closing of a New York City television channel that broadcast worship services, gospel music shows, theological discussions and aired extensive coverage of the Pope's visit to Mexico and St. Louis. The opportunities for these religious shows were open to all denominations. They were being replaced with tourist information, weather reports and coping with emergencies. This decision closed out a superb record, quantitatively and qualitatively, of religious programming in a climate of interfaith coalitions. The decision was met with weak protests from representatives of all faiths.

"It sounds, Bill, like a decision that is extremely secular in its origin and intent. It is sad that the listening audience of the station didn't speak out as one voice using some of the principles of the *Church in the Modern World*, to give some balance to the decision making process. The social, the human construction of the world, is not secular in the sense of being outside of God's plan, but it is intimately involved with the dynamic of the reign of God. Therefore, we have to be ever alert and responsive to any efforts that reduce or eliminate a focus on God and particularly opportunities for theological discussions that link faith and justice as a necessity."

You know, Jesus, I have to try to identify the wide scope of the issues. I have to influence our brothers and sisters to carefully examine the media, not as a narrative—period, but rather from the standards of Judeo/Christian social justice values. I hope and pray to convert hearts, hearts that sometimes seem very cold. I have to link my faith to the social ills of corruption, anti-Semitism, religious persecution in the church, arson, guns, racial discrimination, the ever widening gap of the haves and the have-nots and housing for the mentally ill. I have to intensify my reading habits to study both sides of the issue from the Catholic Social Teachings viewpoint, and then become a voice joining with others to effect change. In the spirit of Subsidiarity I have to strive to solve our problems at the lowest level possible. Of course, the Church leadership, clergy and laity have a priority responsibility to provide the theological education and training. We don't seem to have learned very much from the ills of this past century. We cannot afford to repeat or continue with the mistakes of wars, persecutions, holocausts, abortions and all the other violence that have been the experiences of the twentieth century.

Jesus asks. "Bill, has society lost its sense of the sacred dignity of every person? Have they forgotten that they are made in the image and likeness of God? Do they understand that both women and men have a prominent place in the social order? You have to teach them that this dignity of the human person can only be recognized and protected in community with others as they always strive to ask the question, on every news item they read or hear: what is this doing to the people"?

I think I am beginning to get a sense of what you are saying, Jesus. Why don't I apply your question to some issues of human dignity in the reality of the world in which we live.

- What does the killing of the infant in the womb do to a life that could have been?
- What does the discrimination against gays and lesbians do to them and to the community?
- What does the opposition to building a shelter for the mentally ill do to them and to the life of the community?
- What does the indifference to the forty million Americans without access to adequate medical care do to our society as a whole and to the deprived?
- What does the beating and subsequent death of an immigrant do to the cause of other immigrants and to the perpetrators?
- What effect does the thousands of homeless sleeping on the cold sidewalks of our cities have on them as individuals and on our society as a whole?
- What is the physical and mental effect on our elderly who struggle for economic survival below or near to the poverty line and to those who are indifferent to their plight?
- What can the life expectancy of our children hope to become

when so many go to bed hungry all over the world, including the United States?
- What will be the long range effect of the Kevorkian climate of assisted suicide or euthanasia on the targeted population if this trend is not stopped?
- What kind of world will the youth of today inherit if they are growing up in environments of poverty and violence?
- What will be the long range effect on the society of today if we continue to be the only country in the first world that executes individuals who have taken the life of another?
- What happens to the future life of a victim of brutality out of a motive of discrimination or worse still, hate?
- What happens to the families of a wage earner who is downsized and forced to leave a decent rate of pay that provides for the basic necessities of life and/or adequate medical benefits in exchange for improvement of the bottom line of the corporation?
- What does history teach us about the survival of nations where materialism and consumerism are the priorities?
- What does sub standard housing do to the lives of the individuals who are victimized by those conditions?

Jesus, I am not trying in my testimony to offer all the answers. However, it is my plea that everyone, prayerfully and seriously, will study the signs of the times. Then, prayerfully and studiously that they will search for solutions by the application of the Catholic Social Doctrine and Teachings. Jesus, up to now such activity for the most part stops with the pastoral letters of our Bishops. Agencies like Catholic Charities, locally and nationally, have picked up on training but the challenge will take more. Help us to develop a whole new line of leadership. Help us to develop a new constituency that will be a strong collective voice of a new Servant Church on the journey to justice for all.

Jesus then suggests; "Bill, why don't you continue with the *Church in the Modern World* documents."

The document was completed in December, 1965. It was six

years after the guerrillas captured Havana in Cuba and Fidel Castro became Prime Minister. It was in the middle of the United States involvement in the Vietnam War. It was four years after the erection of the Berlin Wall, which separated East Berlin and West Berlin. In 1963 the first human traveled in space around the earth. Two years prior President Kennedy was assassinated as Cuba threatened us with missiles. Race riots home and abroad served as a back drop to the publication of the document.

"You seem to be saying that people are not hearing too much about the document. It is so pastoral. It is so contemporary. It is the answer to my Church being the Servant Church, the church of, with and for poor people." As Jesus seems to be encouraging study of the document.

Jesus, it all sounds like a good follow up to the previous testimony where I reflected on the council document on *The Church*.[61]

Jesus comments, "Whenever I prayed to the Father that we would all be One, I was cherishing a feeling of deep solidarity with all men and women, with the whole world. The Council in its deliberation and inspired conclusion had in mind the entire human family seen in everything that envelops it."

Well, you know, Jesus, the world is so perplexed and troubled about so much of what we have discussed earlier. What can be done? It is so overwhelming.

Jesus replies. "Why don't you look for the answer to the question in what you and I have been doing during these days together, namely dialogue. The Council felt there was no better way to show our solidarity in compassionate respect for the whole family than in dialogue in which the problems are brought to the table and discussed with full respect for people with different points of view."

Jesus, there is no reason we shouldn't do that, nor any reason we shouldn't be comfortable doing it. Hopefully, I am not moti-

....

61 Ibid, Chapter 11

vated by any earthly ambitions. I certainly hope not. I am interested in only one thing, to carry on your work under the guidance of the Holy Spirit, to bear witness to the truth. You came to save and not to judge, to serve and not to be served. I must do likewise. We must be the Servant Church.

Jesus goes on, "You mentioned earlier, Bill, the various issues that surfaced as a result of the thirty day vigil for injustice. You know that this should be more than a nice research project. It should be more than just a nice thing to do. This is a responsibility that I have left in the hands of the Church. The Church, clergy and laity should constantly read the signs of the times in which they live and relate them to the Judeo justice values that were taught by the prophets before I came to earth. They should relate them to my teachings during the three years of my public life. They should relate them to the teachings of the Church in the period since."

Well Jesus, I recognize the need to continue to do it. We have not seen the last of economic, social or political injustices, violence, discrimination and the constant threat of total destruction.

Jesus once again affirms the need for prayer; "So you see how important prayer is to the mission. The people of God must have faith to believe that in the openness of incessant communications with God they will be strengthened, discerning and led by my Spirit to the will of the Father."

Well, Jesus, it seems as though I have to repeatedly remind myself of my own human dignity and of the human dignity of every living person. I have to repeatedly reflect on the theology that everyone including myself is very good.[62] At the same time I should always remember the reality of the existence of an evil spirit that produces a struggle on social problems between right and wrong, between light and darkness.

Jesus replies, "As the Second Vatican Council taught, each person enjoys the dignity of a moral conscience pulled by the en-

....

62 Genesis 1:31

ergy of love to avoid decisions that are wrong and doing what is right under God's law and judgment."

Thank God, with your grace, Jesus, we are free to make the right choice. Yes, is it not by that choice we will be judged!

Jesus, the teacher, reminds us to go back for a moment to the subject of the dignity of every person and how that dignity rests on the truth that everyone is called to communion with God. "So, in your education efforts, teach your brothers and sisters that they exist because the Father has created them through love and through love God continues to hold them in existence. You know, Bill, by my Incarnation as the son of the Father I united myself with each man and woman. I worked with human hands. I thought with a human mind. I acted with a human will and I lived with a human heart. So, when a person struggles, say with acceptance socially, or fraternally with a person of different ethnic background, encourage them to reflect on my humanity. Encourage them to act as I taught and acted. Make me their model and follow me."

Thank you, Jesus, for that guidance. Too often, I sincerely and devotedly participate in the Sunday liturgy as you did in the synagogue on the Sabbath. But, the difference comes the other six days of the week. You went out to confront the authorities where there was injustice. I, for whatever reason, often fail to stand up to the authorities to correct the injustices that are swallowing us up. Many times it is in very subtle ways. Perhaps, it would be helpful to us, Jesus, if you would speak a little about the subject of the Common Good I hear mentioned sometimes.

Obviously a subject close to his heart, Jesus replies. "Do you remember when I was on earth I told the leaders that 'the Sabbath was made for man and not man for the Sabbath'?[63] The expression for the Common Good has deep biblical roots as well as it received deep attention by the Second Vatican Council. In respect for the sublime dignity of every man, woman and child that we have men-

....

63 Mark 2:27-28

tioned so many times in this testimony, they should have ready access to all that is necessary for living a genuine human life. This means access to food, clothing, housing, the right to freely choose their state of life and set up a family, the right to education, work, to a good name, to respect, to proper knowledge. They also have the right to act according to the dictates of conscience to safeguard their privacy and rightful freedom even in matters of religion. As you approach the eve of the next millennium in order to implement the attainment of these Common Good objectives, there will have to be a renewal of attitudes and far reaching social changes. Respect for the human person was in the days of the Council and is in the present days a topic that is practical, a topic that is urgent. You must look upon your neighbor as another self without racial exceptions, without any color exceptions, without any religious persuasion exceptions and without any geographic exceptions."

Jesus, it is so easy to hide behind the miles that many times separate us from grave injustices. What comes to my mind on this subject is a recent conversation I had with a friend of mine at Catholic Charities, Ronald by name. Ronald is from Haiti, son of a Navy father and a mother who is a nurse. Ronald highlights a number of problems that focus on why Haiti is the poorest nation in the world. A nation where eighty percent of the population is illiterate, jobs are scarce, housing is in too many cases a cardboard or mud hut which if not fenced in it will be lost to squatters. Garbage and human waste disposal are major problems of health maintenance. If one were to have a serious cut you can only receive medical assistance at the local hospital if you bring your own bandages. The population suffers with serious imbalances of their currency value versus our dollar. The lucky ones who do have the fortune of work opportunities can make baseballs for our leagues, major and minor, for a wage of two dollars a month. Ronald devotes his full time to a compassionate response to the needs of his brothers and sisters who, in some cases, may have experienced persecution there only to find other doors here in the United States to be closed to them.

With a warning, Jesus replies. "Each person must apply the criteria of the Common Good to every brother and sister, regardless of how far and away they are, for if you don't, you run the risk of stumbling into the role of the rich man who ignored Lazarus the poor man."[64]

You know, Jesus, there are two other stories that might help our listeners in bringing them a little closer to the opportunity to touch the pain a few thousand miles away. John[65] gave up all the luxuries and comforts as an attorney on Wall Street after seven years, in exchange for seven years working with the refugees in Cambodia. It would take volumes to tell the whole story. Maybe, someday, he too will dialogue with you about those experiences. But for now, there is one experience that might bring us a little closer to the pain through your eyes on the Cross. A chief magistrate of Cambodia raped a Cambodian woman. The incident was witnessed by one of the his deputies. After a struggle of conscience he chose to testify to what he witnessed. The chief magistrate was convicted and sentenced to jail. Today, the chief magistrate looks out from a prison cell on the deputy who practices law in the village.

Jesus comments; "You don't have to personally go to Cambodia. You do have the opportunity and as my disciple you have a duty to stand up with my Truth and challenge your elected representatives as a participant in a collective voice in the community for change wherever there are violations of human rights."

Anthony[66] shared one of his experiences in Angola with me. How often in the past several years Angola has been brought into my home in the evening news. Did it put any compassion in my

....

64 Luke 16:19-31

65 John Bingham, Director, Immigrant Services, Catholic Charities of the Diocese of Rockville Centre

66 Anthony Mullen, Director of Education and Training, Catholic Charities of the Diocese of Rockville Centre

heart? Another question is whether or not what I hear is credible. Try this! The Catholic priests were feeding three to four hundred people a day. Massacres of the innocent were not uncommon. One time thirteen victims were buried without coffins in an open, common grave. Memories of recent events in Kosovo repeat the story. Brave villagers, who recognized Catholic Social Justice Teachings, moved the bodies to a safe place and built individual coffins as witness to the human dignity of the person. Then, in that dignity, they buried them in individual graves. It was not uncommon for as many as five hundred children to attend the Eucharist within hearing distance of gunfire. In the midst of this danger to their lives, the children were shuttled in two jeeps from their homes to the church and back home. One home was thirty miles from the church. The priests provided the sacraments. They provided the transportation. Jesus, was not the healing of the baby who was dying because of inadequate medicines, the result of the prayers of the villagers for your intercession? Six years later he is a healthy six-year old. It is not easy to debate the question as to why the United States is present. Is it to keep the peace or to protect the huge oil reserves? The presence of your priests requires no debate. They were there at the height of the civil war after the Portuguese left the country. They had the opportunity to leave on the last plane out of this war torn country. The gratitude of the villagers was so beautifully expressed when the last plane flew over the church and a man said to your priests, "thanks for staying with us."

"What do you learn from all this"? Jesus asks.

Well, Jesus, isn't it a similar lesson to John's story?

Most of us are not called to be physically in Angola or Haiti or Cambodia. We can stay with those villagers in Angola or elsewhere through our prayers for peace, through our knowledge and understanding of the issues and our collective voices being heard in the halls of Congress to do what our consciences dictate as being right. This is why we cannot build up walls of indifference or isolation.

Jesus comments. "That is pretty inclusive." He continues to teach us. "You must remember again that this document is the twenty-two hundred bishops from all over the world speaking under the guidance of the Holy Spirit as they are the voice for the voiceless as they come to their aid in a positive way:

- an aged person abandoned by all.
- a foreign worker despised without reason.
- a refugee.
- an illegitimate child wrongly suffering for a sin he/she did not commit.
- a starving human being who awakens our conscience by calling to mind my words; 'As you did it to one of the least of these my brethren, you did it to me'."[67]

When one thinks seriously about the number of possible offenses against life itself the list is mind boggling, isn't it, Jesus?

Jesus replies. "It is more than mind boggling. In the words of the bishops at the Council, 'It is criminal'. These acts of violence poison civilization. They debase the perpetrators more than the victims and oh how they militate against the honor of the Creator. As you mentioned, Bill, the list is long: murder, genocide, abortion, euthanasia and willful suicide which are all offenses against life itself. Then, there are the ones which are all violations of the integrity of the human person, such as mutilation, physical and mental torture and undue psychological pressures."

Jesus, what about other offenses against human dignity? I think of some that are global. Some are right in our own communities. They come right into our homes via the television, the newspaper and now the Internet.

Jesus replies. "Both have to be your concern. They would include subhuman living conditions, arbitrary imprisonment, deportation, slavery, prostitution, the selling of women and children, degrading working conditions where men, women and chil-

....

67 Matthew 25:40

dren are treated as mere tools for profit rather than as free and responsible persons."

Yet, it is very difficult, Jesus, to love the perpetrator in this long list of so called neighbors.

Jesus tries to help. "It is easy to understand where you are coming from on expressing that difficulty. But, the bishops are expressing my teachings when they invite you to try to understand the perpetrators' ways of thinking through kindness and love. Then, it will be easier to dialogue with them. Obviously, not at the expense of the Truth and goodness that you as one of my followers must always proclaim."

Jesus, I hear you but it is still confusing.

Not discouraged with my slowness, Jesus continues. "You must distinguish between the error, which must always be rejected and the person in error. Remember that the person in error never loses his or her dignity as a person even though he or she flounders amid false or inadequate religious ideas."

You are reminding me, Jesus, that God alone is the judge and searcher of hearts. For example, this reminder might be helpful to those who discriminate against gays and lesbians solely because of their lifestyle.

Jesus replies. "How true. If you reflect on my teachings in scripture you will find that you are forbidden to pass judgment on the inner guilt of others."[68]

Now bells are beginning to ring. You taught the great crowd from Galilee, the Decapolis, Jerusalem, Judea and beyond the Jordan that they should love their enemies, do good to them that hate you and pray for those who persecute and calumniate you.[69]

Jesus then goes on. "Invite your brothers and sisters to develop their own issues. Suggest that they identify issues that are global, national, and local. How many of them reflect social or cultural

....

68 Luke 6:37-38; Matthew 7:1-11 or 14:10-12

69 Matthew 5:43-44

rights on the grounds of sex, race, color, social conditions, language or religion? Every one that you identified is incompatible with my Father's design."

Well you know, Jesus, I often hear how busy people are with their everyday activities. Is this really a priority for the average, ordinary person? Why not leave the responsibility with the bishops? They seem to have been very thorough with this Church in the Modern World document.

Jesus replies. "Bill, you seemed to key some of your subject titles around Challenge and Change. At one point in time you mentioned your personal restlessness about the slow movement of theological education and training on social justice issues. One of the many obstacles we face is an acceptance by every person that it is their sacred duty—may I say that again—it is the sacred duty of everyone who claims to be one of my followers that social obligations should be recognized and observed as such without any geographic restrictions. My grace is there to help them to practice moral and social virtues and foster them in social living."

I ask; but, what will bring about a renewal of attitudes that you referred to earlier in the fast pace of materialism and consumerism that is the experience of the signs of the times in which we are living? Again, what will move us beyond our commendable level of actions in charity to a new height of justice, distributive justice, God's justice?

In reply, Jesus continues his direction to me. "Follow me as your model. Develop a disciplined prayer life, a listening prayer. Be detached from everything that stands in the way of justice for all. Become attached to the spirit of God who in wondrous providence, directs the course of time and renews the face of the earth and will assist every commitment to this development."

Jesus continues. "We should move on to the remaining subject matter of the *Church in the Modern World*."

That is fine. As you know, Jesus, the document covers a spiritual wealth of other subjects that should be included in the curriculum of any planned educational efforts on social justice and the role of the Church in this next century. The Council recognized the need to instruct men and women once they were made aware of this sacred duty. We have immense resources available to us for employment in this training. Above all, we must be concerned with our future leadership. I am referring to our youth, our youth who come from all different social backgrounds.

Jesus comments. "As I look out at the world today my teachings seem to have been removed from the dialogue. When I was reading about Kosovo I wondered if I had been mentioned just once in the conversations between NATO leaders, their supporting countries and the Serbians."

I ask you, Jesus. Last night while I witnessed the live bombings, am I any different than the crowds in the Coliseum two thousand years ago?

"Bill, perhaps you and your associates should consider, as others have, a Jesus Christ.com."

We will. Going on, what did the bishops at the Council feel was the problem?

Jesus replies. "They recognized that the world was moving towards one single community. They also recognized that man/woman now produce by their own enterprise many things which in former times they looked for from heavenly powers. The magnitude of this immense enterprise involving the whole human race raises many questions. 'What is the meaning and value of this feverish activity? How ought all of these things be used? To what goal is all this individual and collective enterprise heading"?

At times it is difficult to hear you, Jesus, with the noise of the traffic. Well, if I understand it, Jesus, shouldn't we go back to the basics, go back to Genesis?[70] We were created in God's image and we were commanded to conquer the earth with all it contains and

....

70 Genesis 1:26-27, Wisdom 9:2-3

to rule the world in justice and holiness.[71] Why don't we stop and have some lunch and continue these thoughts.

"Fine," as Jesus continues, "that is exactly why I asked if my teachings were part of the peace negotiations or are you trying to solve everything on your own? My teachings won't inhibit them. On the contrary, they will be an incentive to truthful solutions."

After we order sandwiches and iced tea, I ask Jesus to elaborate a bit more on this subject.

"Yes, I am happy to do that. As you know, human activity proceeds from man and woman. It is also ordered to them. When one works, not only does one transform matter and society but also one fulfills the self. One learns, one develops their faculties, and emerges from and transcends their very self. This, I know, is what those of you who are involved in the Social Justice Mission are trying to do. Another way of expressing it would be to say that you should be engaged in the development of the person. Rightly understood, this kind of growth is more precious than any kind of wealth that can be amassed. It is what a man or woman is rather than what he or she has that counts."

Jesus, how would you weigh the scales between technical progress and the human development?

Jesus replies. "The technical progress is of less value than advances towards greater justice, wider brotherhood, wider sisterhood and a more humane, social environment. Certainly, the technical progress may supply the material for the development of the person but it is powerless to actualize it."

You are aware, Jesus, that the Russians aboard the space ship, Mir, released a satellite of mirrors which as it circles the earth reflects the sun down to earth. Technology wise, it is a fabulous experiment. Humanity wise, wouldn't it be better if it reflected for all to see the problems to be addressed in the development of people?

"Bill, you should have respect for any advances in technology

....

71 Wisdom 9:2-3

that help in the development of people. Do you have any other thoughts"? Jesus asks me.

Having finished our light lunch, we resume our travel to the Hamptons, as I continue the conversation. Parish communities that are well financed have an opportunity—really an obligation. They should help the poorer parishes who are in debt. If we as a church are going to advocate for eliminating the world debts of the poor nations then we should start the example in our own inner circle of the active, faithful as an example to others.

That reminds me, Jesus, of the time Saint Mary's parish community in East Islip gave eight thousand dollars to help in rebuilding the burnt out neighboring Episcopal Church. That was a beautiful example of ecumenism.

It also brings to my mind the full-page advertisement that appeared in our Long Island newspaper, under the title, *The Truth Is Out There*. The copy goes on to hint "that there are murmurs of existence of civilization on other planets and individuals are being invited to use their computers to help scientists do extraterrestrial intelligence." The Father has encouraged the exploration of the unknown seas, land and skies since the beginning of time.

Jesus wants to keep moving. "I am not trying to jump ahead of you but it seems as though you have a concern that this kind of function has a priority over or even indifference to discovering my truth which is just waiting to be discovered by so many that have never heard it. The whole of human history has been the story of dour combat with the powers of evil, stretching from the very dawn of history."

Can one not add in a prophetic climate that the battle will go on until the last day? How can we bring an end, Jesus, to this very unhappy situation?

Jesus replies. "All of these human activities which are daily endangered by pride and inordinate self love must be purified and perfected by my Cross and Resurrection. Then, being redeemed by me and made a new creature by the Holy Spirit, man and woman can love all the things of the Father's creation. Bill, not only can but they must, for it is from the Father that they have received them and it is as flowing from the Father's hand that he looks upon them and reveres them."

Jesus, what about the death penalty for convicted killers? Do they not deserve to lose their life in exchange for the life they took?

Jesus replies. "You criticize China and rightly so for violations of human rights which sometimes result in death. As you know, in the United States, the only western democracy where the death penalty is legal since 1976, there have been five hundred individuals executed and thirty-five hundred more sit on death row waiting for their final day on earth. Defend human life-don't destroy it. Leave the judgments to God."

That raises a related question as I hear you, Jesus. Too often the accused do not receive adequate legal counsel. There have been cases where innocent persons have been executed. We should review the financial remuneration for public defenders. Any person who seeks after peace and justice must carry a cross, which the opponents will place on our shoulders. That was the example you gave us, Jesus.

"Bill, when you have spread the fruits of your nature and your enterprise on earth, that is, human dignity, brotherly, sisterly communion and freedom, according to my command and in the spirit, you will find them once again. They will be cleansed this time from the stain of sin, illuminated and transfigured, when I present to my Father, an eternal and universal kingdom of 'truth and life, a kingdom of holiness and grace, a kingdom of justice, love and peace'. Here on earth, the kingdom is mysteriously present, when I come it will enter into its perfection."

Jesus, thank you for re-energizing my faith. Strengthen my courage to respond. Give me the grace of patience as I await this promise of the divine ending. There are five questions I would like to ask you, Jesus, before I move on. They are all part of the Church and the modern world. Up to now, we have been talking about human dignity, the community of humankind and the deep significance of human activity.

Jesus replies. "The Council established those factors as a basis for discussion centered on the relationship including a dialogue between my Church and the world. The council made worthy note of:

- a fact open only to the eyes of faith that the earthly and the heavenly city penetrate one another.
- a fact that it will remain a mystery in our human history harassed by sin until the perfect revelation of the splendor of the sons and daughters of God.
- a fact that the Church casts the reflected divine light over all the earth, notably in the way it heals and elevates the dignity of the person, in the way it consolidates society and endows the daily activities of men and women with a deeper sense of meaning."

"Sorry to interrupt your questions. Go on Bill."

Well, Jesus, when I go back to the many examples of touching the pain that I related to earlier, the James's, the Julius's, the Fred's, the teenage twins, the widows, the transitional shelter for the homeless and the accompanying support of so many individuals sharing their baptismal gifts, I might say I tried to put flesh on the Council teachings. The first question: Did the Council have anything to say about what the relationship with other churches or synagogues should be?

"Yes, Bill. The Council recognized and valued what other Christian Churches and ecclesial communities have contributed and are contributing cooperatively to the realization of this aim."

Jesus, this brings to my mind, the fact that the Council was convinced of the value the mission can receive from the world in doing the ground work for the Gospel, both from individual and from society as a whole, by their sharing of their talents and their activities.

"Bill, is there any practical experience that you have had that might, to use your expression, put some flesh on this subject"? Jesus asks.

Yes, Jesus. It brings to mind the composition of a Parish Social Ministry Advisory Board that was formed back in 1983. There was a diverse Board consisting of individuals from the medical and legal professions, business, government and persons who had been served. They were a mix of men and women, a mix of Catholics, a Protestant minister and an owner of a local retail store who was Jewish. This diverse group worked so well together as they brought Judeo/Christian social justice values to life in the community.

"What is the second question"? Jesus asks.

What did the Council say about what the church had to offer to individuals?

"By the very presence of my Church it can raise in the minds of men and women, anxieties about the meaning of one's life, of their activities and ultimately their death. The Council affirmed that the most perfect answer was to be found in God alone, who created man and woman in his own image, redeemed him or her from sin."

Jesus, then that would lead to the revelation in your becoming man as the Divine Son of the Father. Then, that leads to you as the perfect model for us to follow. When I do I become more of a person. I reduce the anxieties about my life, my activities, my death.

"So very true. The Council also confirmed that there is no human law, so powerful to safeguard the personal dignity and freedom of man and woman as the gospel which I entrusted to my Church." Jesus centers on the importance of the Gospels.

Jesus, why is that?

Jesus responds with five reasons.

"Why?

The gospel announces and proclaims the freedom of the child of God.

Why?

It rejects all bondage resulting from sin.

Why?

It scrupulously respects the dignity of conscience and its freedom of choice.

Why?

It never ceases to encourage the employment of human talents in the service of God and men and women.

Why?

It commends everyone to the charity of all."

What a perfect fit for everyone who is currently involved in the social justice ministry of the Church. What a perfect basis for an invitation to those who are not active in the inner circle or in the outer circle to come in.

"Go on to the third question." Jesus asks.

Jesus, what does the Church have to offer to society?

"I want to remind everyone again that when I speak about the Council I am referring to twenty two hundred bishops from all over the world convening for two and one half years under the inspiration of the Holy Spirit, the advocate I promised would come after I returned to the Father. You have to occasionally remind yourselves of this so you don't get caught up in some form of secular humanism. Now, we'll get to the question and answer. The Council called upon the Church, not only from the standpoint of its ability but as an obligation, if times and circumstances require it, to initiate action for the benefit of all men and women, especially those in need, like works of mercy and similar undertakings."

Jesus, I hear so much about unity these days. How does that fit into the findings of the Council?

Jesus replies. "The Council again affirmed the encouragement of unity as it is in harmony with the deepest nature of my Church's mission for it is in the nature of a sacrament, a sign and instrument, that is of communion with God and of unity among all men and women."

Jesus, what I am hearing is that the Church can have a real impact on modern society by our effective living of faith and love, not by any external power exercised by purely human means.

Jesus affirms a Servant Church with: "The Council said it well when the statement was made that the Church desires nothing more ardently than to develop itself untrammeled in the service of all men and women under any regime which recognizes the basic rights of the person and the family and the needs of the common good."

Two more questions and I will leave the *Church in the Modern*

World with prayerful hope that this testimony has whet the spiritual appetites of those who will hear it and in so doing they will be graced to become an active participant through listening prayer and then an active voice for change. Jesus, what does the Church offer to human activity through its members?

Jesus responds with a caution; "It is a mistake to think that because you have here no lasting city but seek the city which is to come, you are entitled to shirk your earthly responsibilities. The Council exhorts Christians as citizens of both cities to perform their duties faithfully in the spirit of the Gospel."

Jesus, what I hear you and the Council saying is that it is a mistake to think that I may immerse myself in earthly activities as if those activities were completely foreign to religion and that religion were nothing more than the fulfillment of acts of worship and the observance of a few moral obligations.

Jesus added; "The Council stated it this way. 'One of the gravest errors of our time is the dichotomy between the faith which many profess and the practice in their daily lives."

Father Fred[72] said it another way. As he addressed the title and content of a book he was writing he said that never again would he separate the two words—faith and justice—and he supported that promise with the title *Faithjustice.*

Jesus added, "it was a joy to hear you in the earlier testimony where you identified the Old Testament—Genesis and the prophets—as a support to the relationship of faith to justice. The Council challenged everyone to follow my example as I worked first as a carpenter, then as a teacher as I confronted the injustices of those times—and in both roles always with the backdrop of an unbroken relationship with the Father in prayer."

Where does the leadership come from to invite more and more individuals into this mission? We seem to look to the clergy.

Jesus replies. "Again, I would like to quote some thoughts from

....

72 Kammer, Reverend Fred ,S.J., Director, Catholic Charities USA

the Council. 'Secular duties and activity properly belong to the laity. They should turn to the clergy for guidance and spiritual strength recognizing that they may not always have a ready answer to every problem.'"

It sounds as though the bishops at Vatican II were stating without reservation that it is up to the lay people to shoulder their responsibilities under the guidance of Christian wisdom with eager attention to the teaching authority of the Church. Is this not all the more reason to support the consideration for an expanded penetrating theological education and training on Catholic Social Justice Doctrine and Teachings? Finally, Jesus, last question, what does the church receive from the modern world"?

Jesus replies. "The bishops at the Council recognized this was a two way journey. One way in the acknowledgment that it is in the world's interest to see the Church as a social reality and a driving force in history. The other way for the Church is to be aware of how much it has profited from the history and development of humankind—the experiences of past ages—the progress of the sciences, and the hidden riches in various cultures."

May I close out the testimony on *The Church in the Modern World* with this thought. Whether the Church aids the world or whether it benefits from the world it has one sole purpose—the coming of the Kingdom of God and the accomplishment of the salvation of the human race. You, Jesus, are the Alpha and Omega. This has been a long ride so I leave you with this question.

"Can a college student live in the 21st century just as you lived"?

1 John 2:5-6

CHAPTER 13

LAITY

Jerusalem, Jerusalem you who kill the prophets and stone those sent to you, how many times I yearned to gather your children together as a hen gathers her young under her wings, but you were unwilling. Behold, your house will be abandoned, desolate, I tell you, you will not see me again until you say, Blessed is he who comes in the name of the Lord.

Matthew 24:37-39

Jesus, we covered so much richness and challenge in the *Church in the Modern World.* I need to take some quality time to review and reflect on it. However, I need the teachings on the document on the laity to complete the picture. I need some divine direction and a graced commitment to the role of the laity in charity and most important in justice. I would welcome your help in how to identify the education and training needs of both the clergy and the laity to adequately and effectively respond to this great challenge to be the Servant Church in the next century. Perhaps, we could drive over to Saint Joseph's in Garden City and spend some time on the document.

"Probably, you are referring to a Second Vatican Council document.[73] I am sorry to say so much seems to be a part of many best kept secrets."

....

73 A decree on the Apostolate of Lay People, Second Vatican Council, November 18, 1965.

How true, Jesus. This is another subject that people say: we never heard this before, why? May I give you a little rest, Jesus? You have had a long day. I'll quote from the document. I hope that our brothers and sisters will be able to reference these words to your lifestyle. You were such a great model for this mission of charity and justice. I quote:

> *Wherever men, women and children are to be found who are in want of food and drink, of clothing, housing, medicine, work, education, the means necessary for leading a truly human life, wherever there are men and women racked by misfortune or illness, men or women suffering exile of imprisonment, Christian charity should go in search of them and find them out, comfort them with devoted care and give them the helps that will relieve their needs. This obligation binds first and foremost the more affluent individuals and nations.*

"There are three points I would like to emphasize," Jesus comments. "One, you will remember that this is twenty two hundred bishops from all over the world, carrying out their teaching responsibility, inspired throughout by the Holy Spirit. Two, how broad the coverage of needs and why it is so necessary for everyone to share their baptismal gifts. Remember when you go back to your communities all of this hurt, pain and brokenness is there. So, there ARE poor in your community. Third, you are being encouraged and blessed to remove the walls of isolation and go out and find the poor."

As you know, Jesus, throughout this testimony I have been striving to affirm the great works of charity that take place in our communities and at the same time face up to the major challenge on the justice subject.

"You did such a good job on the charity quote from the Council. Why don't you complete it"? Jesus requests.

Thank you, Jesus, and I will. I quote:

> *If this exercise of charity is to be above all criticism and seen to be so, one should see in one's neighbor the image of God to which he or she has been created, and to you Christ Our Lord to whom is really offered all that is given to the needy. The liberty and dignity of the person helped must be respected with the greatest sensitivity. Purity of intention should not be stained by any self-seeking or desire to dominate. The demands of justice must first of all be satisfied; that which is already due in justice is not to be offered as a gift of charity.*

Since I know this so well I interrupt and ask everyone to give your undivided attention to the challenge that follows. Herein lies the core of to touch the pain, the challenge for justice for the next century.

"Go on, Bill." Jesus says.

I quote:

> *The cause of evils and not merely their effects ought to disappear. The aid contributed should be organized in such a way that beneficiaries are gradually freed from their dependence on others and become self-supporting.*

Here again, I would like to make a couple of comments. There are a multitude of problems that individuals bring to our Outreach and Vincentian volunteers that can result in change through the willingness of the individual to strive for the change and the compassionate concern of the volunteer. Some examples would be alcohol/drug addiction, unemployment, housing, a prescription, food, clothing or loneliness. However, there are many types of problems that no single volunteer alone with the hurting person can bring about change. Examples would be low income housing, access to medical care, violence in the streets, racial discrimination, fair wages, decent working conditions. These problems exist in our communities, in our states, in our nation as well as globally. The television nightly news or the Internet will confirm it. This requires a collective voice of the community for change.

"I hope before we conclude with all of the material you have gathered, you will make suggestions for consideration as to what should be done to implement my mission in the contemporary world."

Later, I will come to a number of specific considerations. For, a conclusion to these comments on the challenge to the laity and their responsibilities related to charity and justice, we also need as a Church, the clergy and religious, together with the grace, the passion, the theological education and training to implement these teachings. For, as we heard, the document clearly states that this obligation binds first and foremost the more affluent individuals and nations.

This was a nice location for this discussion on the challenge to the laity.

"Very appropriate," Jesus agrees and concludes the dialogue with this question.

"Can an individual who is blessed abundantly with this world's goods live in the twenty-first century just as I lived two thousand years ago"?

1 John 2:5-6

CHAPTER 14

CHANGE

> *The way we came to know love was that he laid down his life for us, so we ought to lay down our lives for our brothers and sisters. If someone who has worldly means sees a brother or sister in need and refuses him or her compassion, how can the love of God remain in that person? Children, let us love not in word or speech but in deed and truth.*
>
> *1 John 3:16-18*

After Jesus gave a homily at the noon liturgy at Saint Catherine of Sienna, we have come to the home of the County Executive for lunch. We want him to be a part of the plan for the future.

Jesus asks. "Bill, what do you want to do with all of this now that we seem to have reached a good point for the challenge as to where do you go from here? You have tried to face up to the realities of the times in which you live. You made an appraisal of the signs of the times locally, nationally and globally. You discussed the challenges that you as a pre-Vatican Council Catholic experienced as well as the challenges the Church experienced in the same period of time. You proceeded to the experiences of the same participants—you and the Church—in the post-Vatican Council years from 1964 to 1982. Bill, those experiences seemed to bring you to the conclusion that everyone, especially the people who would say yes to an invitation for active participation in the Social Justice Mission should begin at the foot of my Cross—an invitation to be a part of the Servant Church."

Yes, Jesus, I was moving towards the right chemistry, so to speak, the complementing components to truly be one of your disciples. I was trying to realistically establish the spiritual foundation as we leave your outstretched arms on the Cross and go out to touch the pain as you did.

"Then, what I heard you say was that you recommended, based on your own personal experiences, a pattern of listening prayer, detachment from the forces that keep getting in the way and attachment to the grace filled energies that develop your relationship with me and your brothers and sisters."

Yes, Jesus, these were first steps, so to speak, for the substantial number of men and women, I feel who are not hearing the message as to how to connect your teachings on charity and justice, particularly justice to their everyday life.

"Bill, do you think that Christianity has failed"?

Jesus, you know the answer as well as I do. Christianity hasn't failed. You promised us that it would not fail. You didn't tell us that it would be easier either. In the world you will have trouble, but take courage, I have conquered the world.[74]

No, Jesus. Christianity hasn't failed. We have failed Christianity.

"Stay with that for a few moments. How have you failed Christianity"? Jesus asks.

I believe there are three strong points to make the case.

- The high survey reported number of 75 to 80% of Catholics and Protestants that no longer see the need for regular worship on Sundays.
- The scope of injustices that exists in our communities, our nations and globally.
- The height of indifference, immobility, or isolation from touching the pain of those people.

....

74 John 16:33

I believe that all of the subject matter in my testimony that I have covered up to this point supports the three propositions.

Jesus encourages me. "Go on. What thoughts do you have as to a solution"?

I think, Jesus, that each person has to work at the solutions depending on their own individual gifts and status in life. Every one can do something if they are in love with you. The inner circle of the 20-25% who are currently active have the opportunities to be pace setters. I suggest that they seriously consider that the justice cross is an important role in being a true disciple of you, Jesus. They will be seen as different in today's culture. They will be an example to the outer circle. The outer circle represents that 75-80% of the baptized Catholics, who, for whatever reason, see no need to be a living part of your Mystical Body. There is another outer, outer circle consisting of the different religious persuasions who represent the break away, the divisions that have been created over the centuries since you were here on earth with us.

"You feel, that unless the appropriate healing and the adoption of my lifestyle take place in one circle at a time, it is not probable that the necessary level of justice energies to effect change will happen"?

Exactly, Jesus. We need a strong, diverse, collective voice to speak for the voiceless. The old ways are not working anymore.

As Jesus listens attentively, "go on with your suggestions."

I must start with that strong, spiritually motivated base. I will use a word that maybe has been lost in our contemporary vocabulary. Maybe, it creates some kind of false fears. The word is holiness. The activity that is union with God. It is an incredible realism that God is in our everyday life.

"Bill, as you have experienced, if you try over a period of time to quietly immerse yourself in me, you will be graced to recognize me when you touch the pain of those around you."

Jesus, maybe I should adopt a modern day slang expression—try it—you'll like it.

"Bill, do you recall what the present successor[75] to my Peter had to say recently about this subject"?

Yes, Jesus. It is right here as I used it continually in my Catholic Charities training sessions out in parish communities.

> *No apostolate exists, no apostolate can exist either for priests or for laity without interior life without prayer without a persevering striving toward holiness.*
>
> *Such holiness is the gift of Wisdom which for the Christian is a particular actuation of the Holy Spirit received in baptism and confirmation.*
>
> *May you all be called to sanctity!*
>
> *You have need of the abundance of the Holy Spirit for accomplishing the new and the original task of the lay apostolate with his Wisdom!*
>
> *Hence, you have to be united to Christ, for sharing in his sacerdotal, prophetic and royal office in the difficult and marvelous circumstances of the Church and the world of today.*
>
> *Yes. We have to be in his hands so as to be able to accomplish our Christian vocation.*
>
> *In his hands for bringing all things to God.*
>
> *In the hands of the eternal Wisdom, for participating fruitfully in Christ's own mission!*
>
> *In God's hands for building his kingdom*
> *In the temporal realities of this world!*

Jesus, I should place this message on the Jesus Christ dot com. I have just discovered there is such a web site. Now, there is an invitation for some creativity—for some new wine.

"Where do you recommend we go next"? Jesus asks.

Jesus, I should go back to the communication that I had with the diocesan bishops in 1992 entitled *We Belong to God.* I was in

....

75 Pope John Paul II

need of some affirmation to proceed with sharing the results of the visits to the pastors. One bishop who had reviewed the entire study was extremely positive. He felt the true spirit of the Council had not been captured out there in the communities and that was what my study was all about. He recommended that I forward it immediately to the Vicariate. There was a time when the bishops were midway in the study review that I crossed paths with another bishop. He acknowledged his interest in the findings, at which time I sheepishly remarked: "Will I be excommunicated"? He responded with a smile. "I like people who call it as they see it." The recommendations that I presented to the bishops were affirmed in their words, namely, "our approach has to be one that incorporates both evangelization and justice" and "the thoughts and documentation which were included in the report will serve as a basis for future discussion."

"Bill, what has happened to that commitment"? Jesus asks.

I have no reason whatsoever to challenge the validity of the commitment. It is also very misleading to say very little. We have experienced the early fruits of both an emphasis on prayer and scripture in *Renew 2000.* We are in the early stages of the *Stewardship* with the thrusts of *Time, Talent, and Treasure.* But, six and one half years later I am still restless. It is a peaceful restlessness around the need to make Catholic Social Justice Teachings and Doctrine the number one education priority on the agenda. My worry is that for the most part it is the choir, the same people who are always so faithful to any call from their church, that are the nucleus of the participants. Have we reached the rest of the inner circle or any of the outer circle?

"I don't think we have heard what those specific recommendations were." Jesus replies.

I should go back to them and also comment on their validity eight years later. In the spirit of my peaceful restlessness, I start with a quote from the report.

> *"We can no longer leave the advocacy efforts to the pastorals of the bishops and church agencies alone. As important as they are for crisis situations, we don't need more food pantries or more shelters. We do need a strong moral force to bring about change in a society that is decaying, a society that appears to have lost a will to preserve our moral justice values or maybe it was never seen as part of being a Christian. In my eleven years in Parish Outreach, I find a hunger for God, which is not evident in the large numbers that are not in regular Church attendance, but it is very evident in those individuals who come to your church for assistance. Recognizing that the stakes are high as we look at the world around us, here are a few recommendations that are offered for serious and prayerful consideration."*

Jesus, it is now eight years of involvement later.

The decaying society is worse.

The hunger for God has not been satisfied by any substantial return to faithful and regular worship activities.

The need for a strong, moral force to bring about change is greater and has to be expanded to all justice issues and not restricted to one issue or limited to issues of self interest.

Going to the specific 1992 recommendations to the bishops:

> *#1 The bishops proclaim as a number one grass roots—community oriented priority, for the remainder of the twentieth century, the Social Justice of Jesus Christ. This could begin with the new liturgical year on the first Sunday of Advent, 1992.*

"What do you identify as the community"? Jesus asks. "What about the Advent schedule"?

It was an error not to identify the community as the PARISH community and all inclusive beyond only those people—the twenty to twenty-five percent who are regulars, the inner circle and the seventy-five to eighty percent who have left, the outer circle. It is now the eve of the new millennium, the twenty-first century, a great time to re-energize as the Advent thought never materialized.

This was my next recommendation.

> *#2 Pastors and priests, on a selective basis, be called to an educational renewal on the Social Justice Teachings of the Church. The seminary could be the location. Highly qualified faculty could be chosen from within or outside the diocese. The faculty should be individuals with a strong faith justice commitment and a high degree of sensitivity to the balance of contemplation and justice education leading to action. This should not be a short, crash effort. If we're serious about this agenda, it could be, for example, forty priests (10%) at a time for sixteen weeks. Sessions would be held from Monday through Thursday with Fridays off and back in the parish for the weekend. This is a bold, unconventional recommendation and yet can we provide the mandated leadership with less? In three to four years every priest would have had this additional training and experience which at present seems to be considered a real need.*

"Do you still feel strongly about this, Bill"?

Yes, Jesus, I do. As a matter of fact, more so than ever and with full respect for the availability of time.

This was one of my early recommendations.

> *# 3 Make an ongoing, conscious effort in every parish of the diocese to teach people how to pray: privately, in small groups and in the larger community. At the same time, starting on the First Sunday of Advent, 1992, ask the people for an ongoing commitment for prayer for the rich fruits of the Social Justice Mission. We should also seek ways in every community to pray with the poor, both Catholic and non-Catholic, on a regular basis. From personal experience over a number of years, this is very doable if we try.*

"Bill, is this really doable"?

Jesus, I am convinced that it is, based on my own personal experiences. This requires an examination of conscience on the part of all concerned. No way am I to run the risk of being judgmental. It is only my intention to suggest and encourage raising the question about the effectiveness of efforts to date, not only qualitative but quantitative. It does take more than the good publicity efforts of signs, billboards and highway activities. It is in order to ask every person who has been a witness to this testimony to first identify whether or not they have a hunger for a deeper relationship with you, Jesus. If the answer is in the affirmative then make contact with your clerical or lay spiritual leaders. If for whatever reason what is being offered does not fit your needs, let's dialogue and let's find a solution. If you feel a call as a result of my testimony please keep the call energized. Stay with it.

"Very interesting," Jesus comments. "You know, my own ministry was not limited to prayer in the community nor to the privacy of communications with my Father. I went out to the people. I taught them how to pray and so many became my disciples. I went out to them and touched their pain and so many experienced a conversion of hearts—so many were healed."

Then, I made this 1992 recommendation.

> *#4 In my diocesan travels, I find many churches closed. Put the gold and silver away and open them up, so that people can enter to pray with our Lord in the Blessed Sacrament. One step further, may a priest be available in the church, a place of reconciliation for an hour or two every weekday to provide and to encourage an expanded and comfortable opportunity for healing of the hurt, pain and brokenness that exists. Develop and expand individual, spiritual direction in every parish community.*
>
> *Interesting! It is now 1999. This point in my testimony coincides with the epistle of today. Peter and John go up to the*

> *temple to pray and meet a beggar asking for alms. Peter replies. "I have neither gold nor silver, but what I do have, I give you. In the name of Jesus Christ, the Nazarean, rise and walk."*[76] *Since I no longer travel around the diocese I have no way of knowing the extent of the closed doors. If there are still some locked doors, as I suspect there are, I would ask for a prayerful reconsideration of the policy. As to the other step, the number of priests has decreased. Yet, remember in the earlier story, where did James go in his greatest hour of need? He came to his church at 6:00 A.M. Where do the hundreds upon hundreds of individuals in need of material assistance come? They come to their Church Outreaches and Saint Vincent de Paul Conferences. Each one has a material need. This is true. But, our experience tells us they also have, and not always so visible, a spiritual need. Jesus, I would add my own personal testimony to the immeasurable fruits and graces of the Eucharist and the sacrament of Reconciliation received at a regular frequency.*

"As you seem to recognize, Bill, this is so important in your healing ministry." Jesus comments. "Are there other recommendations that you made to the bishops"?

Yes, Jesus. There were, as a matter of fact, eight more.

"Then go on." Jesus encourages. "May I hear them"?

1992 Recommendation #5 was to:

> *Believe that the same priest who has the God given power to change bread and wine into the Body and Blood of Jesus, has the God given mandate and power to lead, teach and guide the laity to change unjust structures for the Common Good.*

Obviously, this is still valid in 1999, Jesus. Only, vocations have decreased while the scope of injustice has increased as the gap

....

76 The Acts of the Apostles 3:6

NA

between rich and poor widens—locally, nationally and globally. This only emphasizes the tremendous need for more trained priests, deacons, religious and laity in the Social Justice Mission. We have to train the trainers.

Directly connected was Recommendation #6.

> *Target Catholic lay leadership individuals in government, business, education, science and the professions for contemplative justice education and action in the communities. The Pastoral Formation Institute, the Catholic Charities Fordham Parish Social Ministry Course, Passage and the Catholic Charities "Open Moment" are small steps, but steps in the right direction. However, if we are serious in our positive response to the call, we must have a determined and ongoing, expanded, grace-filled effort and commitment in every community.*

"What has happened in those specific functions you mentioned"? Jesus asks.

Well, some of them no longer exist while some others have been replaced with different efforts. Jesus, the efforts that remain are very good in of themselves but for a real conversion of hearts in great numbers we need more depth in content in a longer period in time if we are to make a difference—if we are to effect change in the multitude of injustice issues. Remember earlier the words of the senator—"Politics is a game of numbers. You have a small constituency. If you want change, go back and educate the people in your community."

"Bill, go on with the other recommendations that you made in 1992."

Recommendation #7 was that:

> *We must encourage ongoing justice dialogue at all levels of the community. In support of this statement we offer the following from the Second Vatican Council Constitution, The Church in the Modern World. "We want frank conversation to compel us all to receive the inspirations of the Spirit faithfully and to*

> *measure up to them energetically. For our part, the desire for such dialogue, which can lead to truth through love alone, excludes no one, though an appropriate measure of prudence must undoubtedly be exercised."*

Jesus comments. "It seems as though *The Church in the Modern World* had a major influence on your own activities."

Yes, it did, Jesus, then and now. That is why it has always been an important subject in my training efforts. It is also the reason I devoted so much time on the document in this testimony.

"Go on to the next one." Jesus requests.

#8 Recommendation was as follows:

> *That there must be an acceptance on the part of the pastor to insist on a full time effort with accountability from all of the parish staff and any other individuals who are engaged in the Social Justice Mission, with special emphasis on contemplative education and contemplative action.*

Well you know, Jesus, I am not sure if I was as clear as I should have been on this one. What I was trying to say then and I urge for consideration now covers two points. One, that there be a full time Parish Social Ministry Coordinator who receives a just financial remuneration and just benefits. Two, that the coordinator be a member of a parish staff that has received the proper training to produce a dedication and commitment to Catholic Social Justice Doctrine and Teachings.

"Bill, I think that is a little clearer."

May I go on, Jesus?

"By all means, continue."

Then, there was #9 where I urged that there was:

> *A need for strong leadership effort to eliminate the dissension and divisions that exist in diocesan, parish and non-diocesan functions directly concerned with social justice. We have to break*

> *down the walls of turf protection and single issue positions and together build our response to the challenge with one focus only. That focus is the sacred dignity of every single human person from the womb to the tomb. Can this really happen without first building an intimate relationship with Jesus? Is this not the key to all change?*

As the luncheon guests sip their coffee, Jesus comments. "Hearing your first step then and your first step in this testimony, your main focus has not changed."

You see, Jesus, how well you have taught me. I have tried to listen to the many instruments you have placed in my path: scripture, spiritual direction, homilies, spiritual readings, examples of your saints and most importantly, the cries of the poor. You must be the center of my life.

"Bless you. Go on now with the remaining recommendations from 1992."

Number 10 was to:

> *Review all diocesan education to insure proper weighting and balance of the diocesan Social Justice Mission as a support structure to the parish communities, namely, schools, religious education, adults and children, and the Pastoral Formation Institute.*

My 1999 Update: I affirm the joint efforts that have been made by the Pastoral Formation Institute and Catholic Charities to effect Public Policy but as mentioned earlier the constituency is too small. As long as pro-choice, pro-death penalty, minority discrimination and/or isolation, indifference to the principles of the *Common Good* exist in the present scope, then the need to go back to the drawing board of justice education should be a top urgent priority. As long as we have a record high number of Catholic men and women in leadership positions whose voices are silent or they take anti-church teachings positions, then, we need to re-examine the social justice curriculum.

Jesus asks. "Bill, is this what you meant when you rephrased the question on Christianity—"Have we failed Christianity"?

Exactly. May I go on with some comments about our youth?

I recommended in #11 that a specially designed ministry for youth be developed with the proper balance of the spiritual dimension and social justice action. This is an integral part of the building of vocations for the priesthood, religious life and lay ministries. Herein lies the church of the future. What kind of world will we leave them?

May I update this subject related to our youth. Jesus, to me, it is a grace filled experience any time I look into the eyes of an infant, child or teenager. Can I, with any sense of conscience, look into their eyes and not be passionately concerned with an honest answer to that question. I tried to address the problem in the identity chapter. The level of our social ills is worse, not better, since recommendation #11 was made in 1992. We can no longer accept the cliché that they are too young to understand Catholic Social Justice Doctrine and Teachings. Nor, can we accept that some charity experience, for example, an hour in a soup kitchen or participation in a fund raising is all that is needed.

Jesus asks. "It sounds as though there is something you want to build on around this subject."

Yes, there is. At Catholic Charities we have had two experiences at two diocesan high schools that are not only worth mentioning but should be serious consideration for not only the other Catholic high schools but the public school student population as well. We have conducted Catholic social justice workshops around different issues at Saint John the Baptist High for four years. Overall, we should affirm the students' positive response and most importantly the leadership of the administration and some members of the faculty in making this possible. The faculty have an obvious great potential as the trainers in this ministry.

Jesus displays his interest in the youth. "Do the students seem to have an interest in further pursuit of the subject matter"?

There was an experience a few years ago at Saint Anthony's in South Huntington that answers your question very well. After nine weeks of forty-five minute sessions with the junior class we conducted a survey at the end of the cycle. One of the questions was directed at their interest in opportunities for further study of Catholic Social Justice Doctrine and Teachings. Thirty-four students out of ninety-seven in total responded with a "Yes."

"Were you able to provide a positive response to their interest"? Jesus asks.

Not immediately due to some administrative snags. But, two years later I was invited back for a number of weeks. Maybe, it is time to move on to the final recommendation to the bishops?

"Please go on." Jesus requests.

It went something like this.

"Wherever I am, there my servant will be too."[77] If we accept that the Church and the poor should be ONE, as Jesus modeled for us, and we are truly committed to the mission, we must free the pastoral leadership from some of the chains that bind them, from the time eaters that take away from their own daily lives and leave no room for the social justice leadership role.

In this year 1999, it would appear from my observation tower that if anything—the chains are more binding, not less. This is based on the ever increasing shortage of priests—one pastor priest parishes and to my knowledge no significant lifting of the burden of administrative and/or managerial responsibilities. If only we could barter those duties for prayer time. Seven years ago I saw the lay parish business administrator as part of the solution to this problem. How much progress since then is a well-ordered question. There were some other recommendations in the spirit of this one, which will be quickly summarized for the purpose of re-examining the progress:

....

77 John 12:26

- that diocesan functions serve the parish—not to be served
- that we have a climate of more diocesan listening—less talking
- that the overload of diocesan communications be reviewed
- that financial and volunteer resources be twinned between rich and poor parishes

My Update: Great News—In the year 2000, eight affluent parishes will ease the debts of eight poor parishes.
(Continuing the summary)

- that the feasibility of professional management companies for a cluster of parishes be explored
- that in all considerations the autonomy of the pastor is fully respected

Jesus, now seven years later I raise the aforementioned questions only as to their being possible deterrents to the main objective of this touch the pain testimony. Namely, Catholic Social Justice Doctrine and Teachings for everyone—not a light touch but a penetrating fire in the belly depth that builds every parish community as a truly Christian community as the Body of Christ. As was mentioned seven years ago and I mention again now, I pray that if nothing else, these thoughts will serve as a catalyst to accept the validity of whatever may be standing in our way. Remove it and move the Social Justice of Jesus Christ agenda to the forefront, to a top priority position for the parish and the diocese—now and on into the unforeseeable future.

"Bill, do you have any further specific thoughts or considerations as to how"? Jesus keeps the conversation on track.

Yes, Jesus. I do. Less than one year ago in June, 1998, the United States Catholic bishops issued a publication under the title, *Sharing Catholic Social Teaching—Challenge and Directions*. This would be an excellent base for:

a) A challenge to every parish and diocesan function as to the to date progress on the implementation of the recommendations of the Bishops and the Tasks Forces.
b) What are the resources that are required, target area by target area, for the implementation to make this now the number one priority in every parish community?
c) The development of a time schedule that ensures the necessary continuity of this effort in a prioritized position in the parish community.

"Is there anything that you would add or delete"? Jesus asks with his continued interest.

Who am I to correct the bishops, but. We all have our share of but's. Early on, I mentioned the proper balance of activities in a parish community that was serious about the commitment to the Social Justice Mission. The balance scales should be equally weighted between Liturgy/Sacraments, Religious Education and Social Justice. I identified earlier my experience in training several hundred individuals. It was the common denominators of spirituality/prayer, Catholic Social Justice Doctrine and Teachings, and touching the pain which almost always produced the same response, namely:

"We never heard this before—why aren't we hearing it"?

They were energized to become involved in some area of charity or justice or both.

I believe there is a void in the bishops' reflections that the spirituality/prayer and to touch the pain are not mentioned. If one were to follow the academic only it runs the risk of being just another program. We don't need more programs. We do need a mass conversion of hearts. We need the senator's numbers to bring life and reality to the Teachings and effect change. This is God's work. If I shut God out I will do some good things in the name of secular humanism. I will not do great things for the glory of God. I am not being called just to pray and learn. I am called to pray, to learn and to touch the pain of our hurting brothers and sisters in Riverhead, on the streets of New York City, in the poverty pockets of the United States and in the global Kosovo and Rwanda. Forgive me, dear Bishops. I am sure you assumed that it was to be taken for granted. But, experience dictates that we too often plunge into the academic without this balance and the results are nice and that is about all one can say. With these points, I rest my case.

"Bill, do you wish to comment on who the target audiences are in a community"? Jesus seems to sense some incompleteness.

Yes, I would be happy to do that now. I will list them in order of importance with maybe a few related thoughts. I start with a backdrop curtain that recognizes the need for inspired and informed leadership in a multitude of areas. A number of the present leaders have to be moved beyond their present, affirmed roles in charity to the void in justice. May I be specific? There has to be a movement of many of the targeted groups from pro choice and pro death penalty to pro life from the womb to the tomb and from discrimination to the dignity of every person. We have to move them from the silence to being an active voice as part of the senators' numbers for change.

To be specific:

PASTORS AND PRIESTS—

"Enable us to recreate our world and restore justice."[78]

DEACONS—

We have to reflect from the experience of five Saturdays, two years ago at the seminary, where thirty-four deacons participated in the Woodstock social justice presentations to the

....

78 Prayer of Renew 2000

NA

present Home Study fifty-two week curriculum with twenty-four deacons. They too, have a hunger for this ordained mission. They too, need in depth education and training. We have to find ways to free them from some of the time chains that bind them, namely, weekend parish duties, their regular work schedules and at the same time enhance their relationships with their families. Not easy, but there has to be a solution. Social Justice is the core of the deacon's mission.

"Enable us to recreate our world and restore justice."

SEMINARIANS—

"Enable us to recreate our world and restore justice."

PARISH STAFFS—

"Enable us to recreate our world and restore justice."

RELIGIOUS—

"Enable us to recreate our world and restore justice."

DIOCESAN BOARDS OF TRUSTEES—

"Enable us to recreate our world and restore justice."

KNIGHTS of MALTA, KNIGHTS of the SEPULCHER and KNIGHTS of COLUMBUS—

"Enable us to recreate our world and restore justice."

LAITY, SENIORS, PROFESSIONALS, BUSINESS—

(the Woodstock group is a good model),
"Enable us to recreate our world and restore justice."

GOVERNMENT OFFICIALS, EDUCATORS—

We also should consider Home Study for all who cannot find time for formal classroom.
"Enable us to recreate our world and restore justice."

COLLEGE STUDENTS—

"Enable us to recreate our world and restore justice."

YOUTH—CATHOLIC AND PUBLIC SCHOOLS—

You are our future.
"Enable us to recreate our world and restore justice."

DIOCESAN STAFFS— "

"Enable us to recreate our world and restore justice."

COMMUNITY LEADERS—

(regardless of religious persuasions)
"Enable us to recreate our world and restore justice."

INDIVIDUALS—

who have left an active participation in Catholicism—
"Enable us to recreate our world and restore justice."

"Bill, you have certainly covered the waterfront with that list." Jesus remarks. "I hope our luncheon host is experiencing a sense of the scope of the justice mission and how government has a responsibility and a role in the implementation."

Jesus, if we are serious about this commitment, over a period of time we believe this is the road to being the Servant Church. This is the road to the Church being the Church of the poor. This is the road to ONENESS with you, Jesus, as the model of prayer, out to the hurting for healing and out to confront the authorities wherever there is injustice. What does your list look like, Jesus?

"Bill, my list is everyone. I would extend this invitation specifically to the prioritized individuals to whom you have dedicated and shared your thoughts throughout this testimony. The active twenty to twenty-five percent who, for the most part may not see this justice agenda as my agenda and those individuals who for whatever reason have left the Church that welcomed them in Baptism.

- Come to the foot of the Cross-where my arms have been outstretched to you.
- You who are now experiencing some kind of hurt, pain, or brokenness, come back with us.
- You who have many or few gifts—God given gifts—come back and share them with those in need.
- Join with your brothers and sisters who are there ready to welcome you back with my open arms.

As together we proclaim the year 2000 acceptable to the Father.[79] Yes, dear brother or sister, dear manufacturing executive, dear postal clerk, dear priest, dear member of the assembly, dear bank executive, dear automobile mechanic, dear supermarket clerk, dear director of athletics, dear housewife, dear inactive religiously, dear college student,

dear whoever you are—wherever you are

if you allow the fusion of my soul with your soul—my mind with your mind—my will with your will—

You can live in the twenty first century just as I lived."

....

79 Contemporary Update Luke 4:16-22

CHAPTER 15
PRESENCE

> The joys and hopes, the sorrows and anxieties of the men and women of our time, especially of those who are poor or afflicted in any way are the joys and hopes, the sorrows and anxieties of the followers of Jesus Christ as well.[80]

Jesus, it doesn't seem possible that for now we have reached the end of this testimony. How this time together has flown. Yet, Jesus, are we not always together? Just as we sit here, you and I, and watch the sun come up over the horizon supported by the blue waters of the Atlantic.

"Yes, we are one and it is to that oneness that I invite everyone."

Jesus, I would like to share some thoughts on the subject of Presence. If at any time I feel it is appropriate to repeat some prior thoughts, allow me to do so. Repetition of your teachings never is wasted. Jesus, I will build "The Vision of the Council Comes Alive" around Presence. I will try to build it also on some theological roots as the foundation. I will move from the old model of the Church, which I referred to earlier, to hopefully some new levels of energy.

Jesus asks. "Where are you turning for your inspiration"?

....

80 Second Vatican Council, Gaudium et Spes, The Church in the Modern World, Preamble

I am turning to the Second Vatican Council, naturally.

"I hope that you will remember from one of our earlier times together to connect your spirituality with my teachings around charity and especially justice. When you do this, the vision should be firmly entrenched in a relationship with me through a disciplined prayer life and quality time balanced with the action to free so many of my brothers and sisters who are oppressed. This oppression is sometimes visible but sometimes not so."

You know, Jesus, during many of my training sessions I would refer to Webster's Dictionary to explain the meaning of the word presence.

"What did you find"? Jesus inquires.

One definition was an intangible spirit or mysterious influence felt to be present.

"Was there another"? Jesus asks.

Yes. It was the state or fact of being in a certain place.

"I am sure that those definitions can be helpful but are you not dealing with a matter of faith—but go on."

I have always found the mystery of creation to be a good place to start and continually reflect on. It becomes a graced experience that brings about a burning intangible fire in one's soul—some mysterious Presence.

Jesus comments. "Before you reflect on the creation of the material world, go back again to the Trinity—to love. Remember, I am present to the Father, as the Spirit is present to me and to the Father. This Presence, this oneness, this love exists before the creation of the wonders of the universe. It is a Presence without a beginning, a Presence that is now, a Presence that will never end."

Yes, Jesus. How mind boggling and as you said it is a matter of faith—what a gift! I have found from experience that frequent and serious reflection on the many wonders of my own creation, minute by minute, helps so much in the development of a relationship with you, as well as all my brothers and sisters. It is so easy to take so much for granted, even one's own creation.

"How do you do that"? Jesus asks.

One way I could suggest is to take the point in time of one's conception, nine months prior to the birth date. Prior to that conception date one did not exist except in the mind of God—more mind boggling!

"For you, yes, not for God. You mentioned the universe. What are those thoughts"?

It is a good subject for reflection time in listening prayer. Time in reflecting on the wonders of creation:

- the celestial bodies: the sun, the moon, the other planets, the stars
- the blue vaults with the mountains, valleys, oceans, lakes, rivers and streams
- the animals, the birds, the fish the person—body and soul—the person every person—all six billion of us.

Jesus says. "Now, why don't you move on to Presence in the centuries before I came down to earth in human form."

Jesus, that takes me on a journey of faith with scripture and tradition as the navigators. I believe that the Trinitarian love was present in every moment of the joy and hope, the grief and anguish of the Chosen People down through the centuries until you arrived in your humanity.

"Are you referring to periods like the age of Noah and the flood, Abraham and Moses"? Jesus asks.

Yes, that love as you know, Jesus, was present to the Jewish people in the Egyptian slavery right up to and including their deliverance.

"Our oneness touched their pain." Jesus comments with compassion.

Jesus, that all seems so long ago. It seems so far removed from here on Long Island on the eve of the twenty-first century.

"Bill, perhaps it will be helpful to refer back again to the time of the prophets, prophets like Isaiah, Jeremiah and Amos. Are there any parallels in the pain of the society of those days with our present time"? Jesus knows that this subject was covered earlier in my testimony but seeks the repetition for emphasis.

Yes, Jesus they denounced the oppression of women, children, orphans, refugees and aliens and prophesied that the society of those days would be judged by the way they treated those people.

Jesus challenges. "Throughout these reflections you have referred a number of times on the injustices that exist in our world today. Bill, do you not think that the society of the third millennium also will be judged by the way the most oppressed populations are treated? And who are they?

- are they not women who struggle for equality in so many places: locally, nationally and globally?
- are they not children in large numbers who die of hunger? Is it not as true in the United States as well as in other parts of the world.
- are they not the orphans who are abandoned by their parents everywhere or the victims of war-torn parts of the world?
- are they not the refugees who came here only to be rejected as our neighbors or the victims of persecution in the Balkans?
- are they not the aliens who cross geographic borders to escape political and/or economic oppression?

Our oneness touched their pain then in the days of Isaiah, Jeremiah, and Amos. Now, in my name, you are being called to touch their pain not only in your community but also throughout the globe. Bill, can you think of some other examples that will help my brothers and sisters to reflect on my Presence, especially related to justice"?

Jesus, you were present to Elizabeth as she carried John the Baptist in her womb.

"Yes, Bill, that is why John 'leaped with joy' in my presence.[81] As you know, he grew up to be a great advocate for justice. When

....

81 Luke 3:10-12

the people asked him 'what they should do' he replied, 'if anyone has two tunics, he or she must share with the person who has none, and the one with something to eat must do the same'."[82]

Jesus, our social justice roots are so deep.

Jesus comments. "The presence of the oneness of love didn't stop there. The Father sent me to take on your humanity and become a model for you:

- in how to live
- in how to suffer
- in how to die

He sent me to show you:

- how to pray
- how to learn from my teachings
- how to proclaim my Gospel by words and example
- how to be present to those in need by your charity
- how to be present to the voiceless in the spirit of justice

In so doing you are melded into the oneness of love as you touch the pain."

Jesus, please go on. You have so much to remind us of in your time on earth. There is so much to help me in the struggle to live just as you lived: you, two thousand years ago, and me, as I enter the twenty-first century. Teach me more about your Presence.

"Well, Bill, as close as I was to John the Baptist in our infancy and childhood, he wasn't sure about my identity in later years. At one point he sent some of his disciples to find out who I was, with the question, 'are you the one who is to come or must we wait for someone else'?[83] I told his disciples to go back and tell him what

....

82 Luke 1:41
83 Luke 18:20

they had seen and heard. 'The blind see again, the lame walk, lepers are cleansed and the deaf hear, the dead are raised to life, the Good News is proclaimed to the poor and happy is the person who does not lose faith in me'."[84]

Jesus, you must have been in some kind of Presence to your Father who sent you here.

"Bill, the Father was with me through the power of the Spirit as I moved throughout the different villages and towns healing and confronting the authorities where there was injustice. Before those activities, the Father and I were always present to one another in my substantial prayer time. Bill, do you think my prayer was always private?"

No. I know from scripture that you were also present to the community when you joined with them to pray in the synagogue. There was one time that I recall where you were an inspiration to all of us who are involved in the justice mission. Perhaps, you might speak to it again for the benefit of the people who are not presently involved or who missed it earlier in my testimony.

"You must be referring to that time I read this passage from the scroll of Isaiah:

> *'The Spirit of the Lord has been given to me, for he has anointed me.*
> *He has sent me to bring the good news to the poor*
> *to proclaim liberty to captives*
> *and to the blind new sight.*
> *To set the downtrodden free*
> *To proclaim the Lord's year of favor'."*[85]

Jesus, what a foundation to build on by translating each word to the signs of the times in which I am now living.

....

84 Luke 7:22-23
85 Luke 4:16-22

:NA

Jesus encourages me. "If there is any serious consideration about involvement, you should find it helpful to do just that. Who are the poor, the captives, the blind and the downtrodden: locally, nationally and globally? Then, you should again prayerfully reflect on the fact that you too have been anointed by your baptism to be present to and touch the pain of the hurt, pain and brokenness you have found."

Thank you, Jesus. Maybe, I could go on. Tell me more about your being present to the hurt, pain and brokenness of your times here on earth.

"I would like to do that and ask you to remember that I was present to so many people. My Presence was inspirational and revered so that a number of men and women made a decision to adapt my way of life. They were so privileged to witness so much. Blessed are all who are unable to witness my bodily Presence except only through the eyes of faith. However, they can witness my Presence in the Spirit as they live out a commitment to prayer, my teachings and action. Now, to go on. How well I remember so many experiences. I was present as I touched the pain;

of the sinful woman as she anointed my feet with her tears
of the multitude as they listened to the beatitudes
of the individuals who learned from my parables

I was present as I touched the pain of the depressed when I told them not to worry or be afraid."

Jesus, were your experiences always so joyful, so peaceful? It seems that way. I can almost feel as though I am there in your Presence.

"No, not always. There were those times when I had to confront the authorities about the causes of injustice that existed. I know that it is an important part of your ministry. Preserve and enhance all the great charitable works but do not be afraid to confront the power seats that cause the injustices."

Jesus, would you give me some examples?

"I am glad to do it. They would be:

- when I rebuked Herod.
- when I compared the people of that generation to the children shouting to one another 'we played the pipe for you and you wouldn't dance.'
- when I condemned the Pharisees with the words, 'you clean the outside of cup and plate while inside yourselves you are filled with extortion and wickedness.'
- when I cried over the city of Jerusalem from the high hillside as the place that 'kills the prophets and stones those who were sent to them'
- when I broke through the false fronts of the authorities by publicly denouncing them as the 'very ones who pass yourselves off as virtuous in people's sights but God knows your hearts'."

Jesus, I remember another time when you challenged their hypocrisy.

"Sadly, it was more than one other time. Was it the time I warned the scribes about walking in long robes and how they loved to be greeted obsequiously in the market squares, to take front seats in the synagogues and places of honor at banquets, who swallow the property of widows, while making a show of lengthy prayers. Yet, the oneness of our love was always there for each and every one of them. If only they would have opened their confused and cold hearts to that love."

That is so unsettling, Jesus. How well I should learn from your warning and be on constant guard that it doesn't befall me as I try to carry out the social justice mission. One hint would be to always remember that in true compassion I always walk at the side of the hurting person. I should never look down upon them with the old wives tale: there but for the grace of God, go I. It should be there with the grace of God, go I.

"Bill, do you think there were times when I felt a void in my

Presence to the Father or his Presence to me? What about the Presence of the men and women who made the choice to follow me? Were they always faithful to me by their presence"?

Jesus, I am not sure of the answers. Help me.

Jesus responds. "First, I will address the question about my Father. There were so many times when in our oneness we were present to one another; for example at the Last Supper

- when I prayed that the apostles would be protected from the evil one.
- when I prayed for you who would come later on and believe.
- when I prayed that the apostles would become one with the Father, with the Spirit, with me.
- when I prayed for your growth in perfection.

Then, there was the Cross. The same Cross where you encourage others to start the social justice mission. You suggest they be present to my outstretched arms now as they were outstretched to my mother, to John, and Mary Magdalene as I suffered and died to atone for the sins of all. Then, there is the presence of my accusers and my executioners: their presence to me and my Presence to them. Father, forgive them for they know not what they do. Bill, do you think there were times when I didn't feel the Presence of the Father"?

Was it on the Cross, Jesus?

"Yes, it was close to three o'clock on that day and in my humanity I cried out to the Father; 'My God, My God, why have you abandoned me'"?

Then, Jesus counsels. "Prayerfully, accept this great gift from me which was so freely given. It is a gift you didn't earn on your own. Rejoice in my Resurrection. Rejoice in my Presence to the apostles. Rejoice in my Presence to the five hundred witnesses after my Resurrection. Rejoice in my glorious Presence to the Father at this very moment. It is the same Presence in the oneness with the Father that has always existed even before the world was created."

What about now? I ask Jesus. When one reflects on the now as reflected in the beginning of my testimony, I might say, where in all of this mess is your Presence. Where are you now? When I say mess, I refer to the corruption, sometimes even corruption in the inner circle, hatred, discrimination, institutional and bureaucratic weakness, oppressions and repressions, wars and death.

"I AM. I never promised you that it would be easy but I did promise you that I would be with you always. I invited you to come into my Presence and bring all your burdens. I promised I would help you carry them as I carried the greatest burden of all time—the Cross. Bill, this has been a wonderful experience. Maybe, it is time to put it all together into some kind of vision, a vision for the twenty-first century. What kind of community am I calling the people of God to for the next millennium? As you try to leave the experience of Presence for the moment in your testimony, remember you cannot really separate, as my divine Presence is always there.

I am there with each and every person who cries out for someone to touch their pain—the hungry people of Kosovo, the homeless men and women who were in the empty lots of Suffolk County last evening, the unwanted pregnant teenagers on Long Island, the men, women and children in our country who do not have access to adequate medical care, the Mexican men who have fled political and economic persecution only to be greeted with not welcome signs on the East End and on and on—I am with them.

I am there with each and every person, who provides food to the hungry, housing to the homeless, and medical care to the uninsured.

I am there with the advocates before the County Legislature, in the Legislative Halls in Albany, and in the Congress in Washington as they speak out with the voiceless for change in unjust systems.

I am there on the Cross.

I am there in the Eucharist, my Body and Blood as their spiritual nourishment."

-Jesus, I pray to the Father in your name that your Presence
will be in every single heart beat of the server and the served.
that your Presence will shine upon us with the warmth of

the rays of the sun.

that your Presence will ignite fires in our bellies as we work for justice.

that your Presence will at the same time be experienced in our souls with the stillness of a pond at dawn, with the silence of a canyon at sundown and with the sacredness of the mystery of your Presence.

"Thank you, Bill. Now, to your thoughts on the vision." Jesus seems ready for this subject.

Well, Jesus, it is a vision of a community and my life in it. It is different than the community I have known. It is a community that includes the faithful twenty to twenty-five percent and those individuals who have left active participation in your Church, the seventy to seventy-five percent who were once a part of the inner circle. It is a community where the inner circle as true disciples with a new to them agenda of justice, reach out to envelop the hurting in compassion, in love, in justice as witness to your eternal Presence.

"But, Bill, don't you run the risk that this might be interpreted as some form of secular optimism or secular humanism"? as Jesus seems to experience some concern.

No, Jesus. It is more around the divine virtue of hope. A hope that finds each person, whether they are in the inner or outer circle, in a divine state of being—in a state of sacred commitment to the challenge of John in his first letter that we have reflected on and challenged periodically throughout this testimony.

Jesus picks up with, "Are you referring to this passage? 'But anyone who does keep my word, in such a one, God's love truly reaches it's perfection. This is the proof that you are in union with me. Whoever claims to remain in me must live just as I lived'."[86]

....

86 1 John 2:5-6

Yes, Jesus, that is it. The reality of the pre-Vatican Council era is gone. This is a new way to most of us.

"Yes, Bill, new to most of your contemporaries but not to me. Remember how I called Simon, his brother, Andrew, James and John? I called them to leave their fishing nets, your earlier detachment subject, and follow me. It sounds to me as though you have a vision of being like the early communities that were formed after I went back to the Father, where the outer circle of those days recognized the inner circle with the words 'see how they love one another'." Jesus suggests that the walls of division be broken down.

This is not easy. There are a number of commitments that go with the vision of a new community. I have to exchange power and prestige for listening prayer and an open heart to your Presence. The vision calls for the destruction of the "we" "they" climate within and without in both circles. It is a vision that transforms the culture of darkness in a very troubled society into John XXIII's Beacon of Light. It is a vision that transforms a bleeding Church in a tortured society[87] into a compassionate, loving church that is totally immersed in the healing of those wounds of society: a Church that is truly the Church of the poor with all their hurts, pain, and brokenness and a Church made up of all the people of God that goes out to touch the pain.

"It sounds, as though the vision is one of diverse individuals in a community who work together to accomplish a common goal and in the process better the lives of my brothers and sisters in need, especially the children." Jesus seems to express his affirmation.

Yes, that is true, Jesus. The vision has at its center, after you, the challenges of the Second Vatican Council to the laity. At this point in the vision I should repeat the challenge.

Namely, wherever individuals are in need of food, clothing, housing, medicine, work, education, the means necessary for leading a truly human life, wherever there are individuals racked by misfor-

....

87 Burghardt, S.J. Reverend Walter J., Woodstock theological Center, Georgetown University, Washington, D.C.

tune, illness, suffering in exile or imprisonment, in Christian charity you should go out in search of them; find them out, comfort them with devoted care and give them the help that will relieve their needs.

"Bill, again, what was it that the Council said about who has the heaviest responsibility for effectively responding to this challenge"?

Yes, Jesus. The bishops first placed this obligation on the shoulders of the more affluent individuals and nations.

"Bill, repeat what the Council had to say to the laity about justice. How does it fit into the vision"?

Jesus, it is really at the core of the vision. It is the heart of my testimony. As I mentioned earlier we really don't need more soup kitchens or shelters. What we do need is the priority for intensive, penetrating theological education and training of the laity, religious and clergy that relates to addressing the causes of the evils and tirelessly pursuing change. The Council is calling for a gradual freeing of people from their dependence on others to a state of self sufficiency—at home and abroad.

"Go on, Bill, with the vision."

The vision calls for a prayer life that cements my relationship with you, with the Father, transforming me into a Spirit led individual, and as I grow in the Trinitarian Presence of love I am led:

- to the presence and bonding with others
- to being more reflective of you in my presence to others
- to a passionate love of the new one circle: You, Father, Spirit, myself, the others, everyone
- to be compassionately at the side of the others
- to letting go of the controls, of the power
- to breaking down the barriers of turf that separate us
- to free myself so that I can free others
- to a posture of preserving and enhancing the great works of charity in the parish communities: Catholic Charities, Saint Vincent de Paul, secular agencies, the unknown numbers in other church communities as we move on to undreamed of levels of justice as we join with others to change theinjustices that bind as they prevent the God intended freedom of every individual no exceptions.

"Bill, this vision sounds like a monumental task. Do you see it for the few or the many"? Jesus asks in anticipation.

Jesus, first of all, nothing is impossible with you. In answer to your question, no, it is not for a few. I see the community in our vision as one where the few individuals who presently carry the responsibility for assistance to the poor, open the gates so that everyone has the opportunity to share their gifts with everyone else. See how they love one another. We are all poor. We all have needs, rich and poor, old and young, healthy and sick.

"Does that conclude the vision"? Jesus queries.

There are four concluding points for the vision. We must establish a priority recognizing that the social justice message must be heard through education and training, through preaching, through collaborative action that will effect change in our communities, in our state, in our nation and around the world. The injustices are so close to us in the Internet, our television and the newspaper.

It is a vision where the powerful and the powerless speak out as one voice after prayerful dialogue with the diverse leadership of the community to effect change through a conversion of hearts, not just minds.

It is a vision that reflects an active role for our youth, the new leaders of the twenty-first century. At age eighteen they can be a voice with their vote.

Finally, the vision sees the destruction of a society that fosters individualism, injustice, tolerance for low standards of behavior, discrimination, apathy and replaces all that with the building of truly Christian, compassionate communities as the Body of Christ.

As the sun, imaging a ball of fire, drops below the horizon, this testimony is concluded. Jesus leaves me with these words.

"Thank you, Bill. May I close with a prayer that, you and all my brothers and sisters will love perfectly and wait patiently as you touch the pain in the twenty-first century."

CNA

90000>
9 780738 819983